MY
BANNER
IS
CHRIST

MY BANNER IS CHRIST

AN APPEAL FOR THE CHURCH TO RESTORE
THE PRIORITY OF SOLUS CHRISTUS
AND TO MORTIFY THE IDOLS OF
CELEBRITISM AND THE
FEAR OF MAN

MICHAEL JOHN BEASLEY

My Banner is Christ: An Appeal for the Church to Restore the Priority of Solus Christus and to Mortify the Idols of Celebritism and the Fear of Man
ISBN: 978-193535-8-10-7

Copyright © 2015 by Michael John Beasley:
Library of Congress Cataloging-in-Publication Data
Copyright Registration Number: TXu 1-967-445
by Michael John Beasley
Includes text, artwork, bibliographic references, and index

For more information go to: www.thearmouryministries.org.

In dedication to

the many saints throughout history

who stood fast in this world

for the sake of the Gospel,

fearless in the face of men

through their love and reverence

for God alone

Psalm 60:4:

Thou hast given a banner to those

who fear Thee,

that it may be displayed

because of the truth.

[Selah].

MY BANNER IS CHRIST

TABLE OF CONTENTS

MY
BANNER
IS
CHRIST

~ INTRODUCTION ~

HE HAS GIVEN

US A

BANNER

In the fourth Gospel, John the Baptist was asked why all were coming to Christ rather than to him (John 3:26). Rather than competing for the attention of the people, this humble forerunner of Christ simply confessed: *He must increase, but I must decrease (John 3:30).* I would submit to the reader that John's reverent confession regarding the supremacy and worthiness of Jesus Christ is one that we all desperately need. After all, pride, arrogance, and self-exaltation are as germane to human nature as is breathing, but the desire to magnify Christ *alone* can only come by divine grace. Apart from such grace, the tendency of human nature is quite the opposite. Man-centeredness is the universal religion of fallen man, and we are all dull fools to deny this. It is for this reason that I say to the reader that John the Baptist's confession of Christ's supremacy and worthiness is the very medicine that our proud hearts greatly need. Without such divine medicine, all that we are left with is the deadly disease of *human idolatry*.

Over the years in pastoral ministry, I have developed an increasing concern regarding the dangerous pathway which leads to the reverence and preeminence of mere men rather than of Christ. By writing on this subject, I make no claim of being above the temptation of human idolatry. It is for this reason that the concerns expressed in this book regarding the church at large, are also concerns that I have for my own soul. As I look back over the years, I can identify several occasions where I was guilty of exalting or fearing men, yet, through it all the Lord has continued to teach me that He alone deserves all reverence, honor, and glory. While attending seminary many years ago, I invited a guest to join me at a chapel service. The speaker was a very popular person whom I admired and respected a great deal. I had already read a few of his books and had heard some of his sermons, thus my opinion of him was already highly favorable. This man preached a sermon in chapel that raised a great deal of controversy among those who heard him that day. He said some things that had many seminary students buzzing with controversy for weeks afterwards. When I heard the sermon, along with my invited guest, I remember feeling a sense of reservation about what he had said, but I quickly ignored any concerns. After chapel I had lunch with my guest who complained about some of the points made by the speaker. I, as a mindless fan of this speaker, proceeded to defend what he said at the chapel service even though I too had private doubts and questions in my own heart. My internal hypocrisy eventually became a rebuke within my soul such that I came to realize that I had placed my love for, and devotion to, one of my favorite theologians over Christ and His word. What at first seemed like a small error of the heart was later revealed to be a well-hidden disease. But this is not all. Remarkably, I was also guilty of the sin of *fearing men.* Aware of the fawning devotion of my fellow seminarians for this famous speaker, I felt a degree of implied social pressure to fall in line with the crowd – and this I did, like a good little fool. I was no victim in this. My choices were a volitional rebellion against the wisdom of Scripture which says, *"The fear of man brings a snare, but he who trusts in the LORD will be exalted"* (Proverbs 29:25). Such mistakes from my earlier days became a sharp warning within my heart, reminding me that all such infractions of devotion to Christ *alone* constitute an incipient disease of the soul – one that can affect myself, my family, my ministry, and my Christian witness in the Gospel overall. In other words, such errors are not minor infractions for anyone, instead they are massive cracks in the foundation of our lives.

I offer this personal account as a means of introducing the core concern expressed in this book. It is my conviction that the modern church has become dangerously distracted from her high calling to *adore* and *reverence* Christ alone. What has tempted and lured her from this precious priority is that forbidden fruit whereby the homage that is due to the Creator is instead directed towards the creature.[1] Such a tragedy as this is guaranteed whenever the church fails to live and minister *in the fear of Christ (Ephesians 5:21).* When *godly fear* diminishes in the heart of the believer, the weeds of ungodly fear will grow in its place, resulting in the corruption of *man-centered fear* or *adoration. Man-centered fear* is evident whenever the creature is seen as having greater authority and power than the Creator Himself. In this context, the dread of enmity with men, persecution, or social rejection will often lead individuals to obey men rather than God. On the other hand, *man-centered adoration* is that corruption whereby individuals are *exalted* and *celebrated* in a manner which diminishes Christ. What is so dangerous about this idolatrous corruption is that it is often quite subtle and unnoticed. Its prominence and popularity in American culture thrives in the modern day, and it is for this reason that I distinguish it with the word: *celebritism.* Its core error is found in the adoration of men over Christ, and its corruption often spreads quickly, especially in this present age of modern media. While there is nothing inherently wrong with the idea of *celebrating* godly men and their ministries, *there is everything wrong with the idolatry of celebritism: the act of exalting men in a way which diminishes the glory and sole authority of Jesus Christ.* The pressures that can lead to this particular problem are enormous, especially in a world which demands that it have its various celebrities and idols: *professional athletes, pop icons, movie-stars, prominent politicians, and even internet-idols etc.,* however, the church must resist such worldly conformity. When it fails to do so, it yields a banner of identity which exalts men rather than Christ, and this is often done under the false assumption that *popularity is a guarantee of veracity and piety.* When such a banner as this is heralded before a watching

---

[1] Romans 1:25.

world, the church's sole Savior, Bridegroom, and returning King is horrifically blasphemed. Scripture never calls us to chase after popular trends or prominent personalities, yet this habit among men flourishes readily in our celebrity culture of the modern era.

The sins of *celebritism* and *the fear of man* both stem from the absence of an *adoration* and *reverence* for God, and every believer must be extremely guarded against this deadly arena of sin. Knowing our human frailty, Satan constantly seeks to lure the God's people into such treacherous territory. Even without his temptations, sinful human nature tends to veer to one such idol or the other like an old jalopy with a defective steering alignment. Left unchecked, this inherent frailty can take any believer off course with little effort at all. All such temptations and defections run rampant wherever there is a lack a genuine fear of God. In such a dangerous condition as this, individuals become far more beholden to the words and thoughts of mere men than they should be. Within this dynamic, it is not surprising that, when teachers of prominence speak, their hearers often slip into a passivity of thought which decimates the requisite *critical analysis* that all believers must have. When this happens, the hearer enters into a dangerous place where the words of mere men are exalted, Christ's authority is diminished, and doctrinal errors can take root in the soul. However, Scripture never grants such passivity to the student of God's word. When we consider the Apostle Paul's own life and ministry, we find multiple examples of this point. For one thing, Paul bore unique authority as an Apostle of Jesus Christ, and yet he never demanded that others follow his teaching blindly and without question. Instead, he called on his hearers to scrutinize his words with extreme care:

Galatians 1:8 ...even if we, or an angel from heaven, should preach to you a gospel contrary to what we have preached to you, he is to be accursed!

By this statement alone, we see that Paul understood a very important principle, and it is one that must be upheld by the church in every age: whatever authority God's servants may be granted in this life, they must remember that Christ is the ultimate authority over *His church*. Therefore, the Apostles and Prophets did not possess any inherent authority within themselves, instead, the authority they possessed came from the Lord.[2] Because of this, God's people throughout history have been called upon to test the veracity of those who claimed to be God's messengers, whether Prophets or Apostles (Deuteronomy 13:1-5, 18:18-22, Jeremiah 14:13-15, Galatians 1:8, 1 Thessalonians 5:19-21). Such reminders as these stand as a rebuke to anyone thinking that exceptions can be made for prominent teachers in the modern era simply because they are *prominent and highly celebrated people*. Even Paul's station as an Apostle did not afford him such a luxury, instead, his teaching was carefully examined by the Bereans such that they "received the word with great eagerness, examining the Scriptures daily to see whether *these things [what Paul taught]* were so."[3] We should note that Luke's record of their activity was not followed with a rebuke against them for some presumed rebellion. To the genuine prophet or apostle of yesteryear, or to the pastor in the present day, scriptural accountability will always be welcomed because such scrutiny reveals the ultimate harmony of God's authoritative revelation, while exposing all imposters to the truth. Because of this, Luke called the Bereans *noble-minded* in view of

---

[2] 2 Peter 1:20–21: 20 But know this first of all, that no prophecy of Scripture is a matter of one's own interpretation, 21 for no prophecy was ever made by an act of human will, but men moved by the Holy Spirit spoke from God.

[3] Acts 17:10-12.

their willingness to measure Paul's teaching by the standard of the very Scriptures from which he *habitually* reasoned:

> Acts 17:1–3: 1 Now when they had traveled through Amphipolis and Apollonia, they came to Thessalonica, where there was a synagogue of the Jews. 2 And according to Paul's *custom* [*eiōthos, habit*], he went to them, and for three Sabbaths *reasoned with them from the Scriptures,* 3 *explaining and giving evidence* that the Christ had to suffer and rise again from the dead, and saying, "This Jesus whom I am proclaiming to you is the Christ." [italics mine]

No matter where Paul preached, he habitually reasoned from the Scriptures, explaining the Scriptures, and giving evidence from them. All such scriptural *evidence* became the standard by which all of Paul's hearers, including the Bereans, could measure his preaching. Clearly, what the Bereans did was not a rebellious response to the Christian faith, instead their noble-minded response was evidence of the Spirit's work within them. Apart from the Spirit, our fallen tendency is to exalt the messenger above his station, while receiving what is said without careful consideration. Such passivity of thought is dangerous. We could list the Roman Catholic doctrine of "papal infallibility" as "exhibit A" amidst a vast warehouse of past and present exhibits of such fleshly thinking. All such reminders regarding mankind's dangerous propensity towards idolatry underscore our desperate need for Christ and His word.

This concern regarding the dangers of *celebritism* and *the fear of man* is something that I have dealt with for many years, and for this reason I have already addressed the subject, *briefly*, in three prior books. Yet, what was a mere parenthesis in those works now constitutes the central concern in *My Banner is Christ.* It should be known, however, that despite the polemical nature of what I have here written, the ultimate design of this book is to direct attention to Christ Himself, remembering that *He must increase, but we must decrease.* In particular, there are three foci that I wish to highlight in light of the title and subtitle of this book:

1. *The Priority of Solus Christus*: The primary goal of this work is to magnify Christ in the church by restoring the priority of *Solus Christus.* Of course, *Solus Christus* is that historic call of the Reformers who sought to magnify the reality that Christ *alone* is the sovereign Lord over all creation and is the church's sole redeemer and head – a central truth that was decimated through centuries through various, incremental compromises along the way. In addition to the call of *Solus Christus* is its necessary companion: *Sola Scriptura* (Scripture alone). These two are inseparable and indispensable, for without the latter, it is impossible to seek the former. Without God's word we do not have the means by which to magnify Christ's supremacy and glory. Moreover, without these two aforementioned *Solas*, all the others fall away: *Sola Fide, Solas Gratias, and Soli Deo Gloria.* The church's daily pursuit must be to magnify Christ's power, supremacy, and authority for He, and He alone, is our message of hope to the church and to the nations. Yet, in order to pursue this priority well, the church must *forsake the idolatry of celebritism, that is, the idolatry of heralding men above Christ.*

2. The Idols of *Celebritism* and *the Fear of Man*: We have already visited the important idea that, wherever the fear of God wanes the exaltation of the creature waxes hot, often igniting the sins of *celebritism* or *the fear of man.* Regarding the term, *celebritism,* I gladly confess that it is an invention. Feel free to peruse the Oxford English Dictionary if you wish, but I promise you that, to date, it is not to be found. In crafting this word, I have taken the liberty of adding the suffix *ism* to the word *celebrity* in order to denote the natural tendency of human excess due to our struggle with indwelling sin. Of course, the word celebrity isn't inherently problematic. At its root, it has in mind the idea of *celebration.* When this word is employed to speak of people, it simply connotes an individual who is *celebrated* for various reasons. However, due to human sin and frailty, *celebrities* are often heralded well beyond reasonable measure, leading to sundry cults, cliques, and factions – various *isms* within society, i.e., *celebritism*. Within the church, it constitutes that grave corruption whereby the reverence and homage that is due to Christ alone is given to mere mortals. Here in America, where religious persecution still remains at a minimum, celebritism remains as a dominant disease. However, as our freedoms continue to wane, we must also remember that the fear and dread of men is an equally poisonous corruption. Like celebritism, the fear and dread of men stems from the sin of *exalting and reverencing the creature above the Creator.*[4] Whatever we may face in the future, we must remember that, whether by fear or fawning devotion, the idolatry of heralding men above Christ is a ubiquitous and deadly disease. This contagion in the church has a long and sordid history, and it must therefore be mortified on a regular basis.

3. The Main Title: *My Banner is Christ*: The science of *heraldry* (a subject that will be further explored in the next chapter) reminds us that banners and flags are normally used in order to signify the identity and authority of individuals, families, institutions, and nations. In the Old Testament, a *banner* [*nes*] was used as "a rallying point or standard which drew people together for some common action…one of the most important being the gathering of troops for war."[5] In Psalm 60:4, we are reminded that God gives a banner of truth *to those who fear Him* so that His glory may be displayed before the nations: "Thou hast given a banner to those who fear Thee, that it may be displayed because of the truth. [Selah]." For the church, she has but one object of adoration and reverence, and only one banner of truth within this fallen world: *the Lord Jesus Christ – who is the way, and the truth, and the life.* Yet the question that remains for believers is this: how well are we clinging to Christ and His authority rather than to false and substitute authorities?

---

[4] Romans 1:25.

[5] R. Laird Harris, Gleason L. Archer, Jr., Bruce K. Waltke, eds., *The Theological Wordbook of the Old Testament* (Chicago: Moody Press, 1980), 1379a.

This question applies for all believers, myself included, and it is for this reason that I ask the reader to remember that the title of this book is not a personal boast, instead, it is an admission that I write as one whose lifelong goal is to have *Christ increase while I decrease*. What I believe and seek for myself, I also seek within Christ's body, and it is for this reason that I issue a heart-felt appeal to the church. By making such an appeal, I must begin with myself, *as we all must do.*

It is my hope and prayer that *Christ will increase* within His church through a renewed pursuit of *Solus Christus,* and through a joyful submission to His authoritative revelation alone - *Sola Scriptura.* I should remind the reader that, though this work contains several polemical arguments, our ultimate resolve will be to seek the biblical solutions to the problems facing the church today. Additionally, as this work was being developed, I was further drawn to the excellent writings of John Flavel (1627-1691) and John Bunyan (1628-1688): two contemporaries who faithfully served as ministers of the Gospel during England's persistent persecution of nonconformist preachers. In particular, Flavel's piece – *A Practical Treatise of Fear* – and Bunyan's work – *A Treatise of the Fear of God* – became excellent helps and witnesses to my own labors. Both of these men strongly grappled with the subject of godly versus ungodly fear during a time of intense pressure to conform with the religious culture of their day. Within the crucible of such affliction, many brethren learned this crucial lesson as summarized by Flavel in, *A Practical Treatise of Fear*:

"...it is far better to lose our carnal friends, estates, liberties, and lives, than part with Christ's truths and a good conscience."[6]

---

[6] John Flavel, The Works of John Flavel Vol III, A Practical Treatise of Fear (London, 1820), 303.

All brethren who have learned this truth through times of testing, illustrate God's gracious and powerful work in the life of frail, human instruments. By infusing the writings of Flavel and Bunyan within this work, it is my hope to introduce some readers to these dear servants whose desire it was to herald Christ in a time which heralded men and manmade religion.

Additionally, it was originally my hope to avoid the matter of identifying individuals by name amidst the quest of describing the struggles of the present day. Knowing something about the sensitivities of many within our celebrity-driven culture, I had hoped that this could be done without destroying the structure of the book's overall development. However, this proved to be impossible. Because of this, I urge the reader to remember the nobility of the Bereans when encountering a critical analysis of any given teacher or teaching. The point is not to tear down people, but to uphold truth.[7] The church is called the pillar and support *of the truth*[8] – not the pillar and support of *prominent personalities within modern Evangelicalism.* Should we lose sight of this distinction, then the priority of having *Christ increase* is utterly lost. The church has no other head or authority and she must therefore rebuff all substitutes for His divine office. When the church understands this truth well, she will be willing to scrutinize every teacher and teaching that comes in her midst – even if the teacher is very popular by the appraisal of the masses. Such activity is not unloving. Instead, it is the most loving thing that the church can do for the Lord and for His people.

Finally, in consideration of this book's title, the importance of reverencing God, along with the priorities of *Solus Christus* and

---

[7] 2 Corinthians 10:3-8.
[8] 1 Timothy 3:15.

Sola Scriptura, I would like to share C.H. Spurgeon's comments on the aforementioned text of Psalm 60:4. The following comes from his excellent commentary on the book of Psalms, *The Treasury of David:*

> *"Psalm 60:4: Thou hast given a banner to those who fear Thee, that it may be displayed because of the truth. [Selah]:* Their afflictions had led them to exhibit holy fear, and then being fitted for the Lord's favour, he gave them an ensign, which would be both a rallying point for their hosts, a proof that he had sent them to fight, and a guarantee of victory. The bravest men are usually entrusted with the banner, and it is certain that those who fear God must have less fear of man than any others. The Lord has given us the standard of the gospel, let us live to uphold it, and if needful die to defend it. Our right to contend for God, and our reason for expecting success, are found in the fact that the faith has been once committed to the saints, and that by the Lord himself.
>
> *That it may be displayed because of the truth.* Banners are for the breeze, the sun, the battle. Israel might well come forth boldly, for a sacred standard was borne aloft before them. To publish the gospel is a sacred duty, to be ashamed of it a deadly sin. The truth of God was involved in the triumph of David's armies, he had promised them victory; and so in the proclamation of the gospel we need feel no hesitancy, for as surely as God is true he will give success to his own word. For the truth's sake, and because the true God is on our side, let us in these modern days of warfare emulate the warriors of Israel, and unfurl our banners to the breeze with confident joy. Dark signs of present or coming ill must not dishearten us; if the Lord had meant to destroy us he would not have given us the gospel; the very fact that he has revealed himself in Christ Jesus involves the certainty of victory. *Magna est veritas et praevalebit (Truth is mighty and will prevail)."*

Such is the overall point of this book: *to unfurl the banner* of *Scripture alone* and *Christ alone* amidst a secular and religious world that has countless competing banners. In so doing, we must remember Christ's victory and triumph over all. By divine grace alone we are the bride of the Lamb and we long for His return. Until He comes again let us raise His banner and uphold the lamp of His word, amidst this crooked and perverse generation.[9]

---

[9] Philippians 2:15-16.

MY
BANNER
IS CHRIST

~ CHAPTER I ~

LESSONS FROM HISTORY

WITH

PILLARS OF WARNING

As noted in the introduction, the Apostle Paul called Christ's church the pillar and support of *the truth*, not the pillar and support of *prominent personalities within modern Evangelicalism.* Should we reverse this truth, by raising a banner for anything else other than Christ and His word, the church would be turned on its head. Sadly, history is filled with examples of such ecclesiastical reversals, yet they serve as important tutors for us in the present. As the reader certainly knows, if we are willing to be good students of it, history can tutor us well in view of humanity's past failings. However, ignorance of history often dooms us to the naive repetition of it.[10] We see this scriptural principle clearly illustrated through the Apostle Paul's warning to the Corinthian church :

> 1 Corinthians 10:11–12: 11 *Now these things happened to them as an example, and they were written for our instruction, upon whom the ends of the ages have come.* 12 *Therefore let him who thinks he stands take heed that he does not fall.* [Italics mine]

According to Paul, Israel's difficult and idolatrous history was recorded *for our instruction.* What he is saying is quite clear: we need the lessons of the past to instruct us concerning our sin and need for grace. Moreover, we must receive those lessons with humility, *lest we fall due to our own sinful pride.* Corinth was a church which evidenced its sinful pride through a host of problems: personality divisions, internal conflicts, toleration of sexual immorality, idolatry, abuse of the Lord's table, and toleration of false apostles among other things. Thus, they were becoming a disturbing reflection of Israel's dark past, and it was time that they looked in history's revealing mirror. By the standard

---

[10] Ecclesiastes 1:10–11: 10 Is there anything of which one might say, "See this, it is new" ? Already it has existed for ages which were before us. 11 There is no remembrance of earlier things; And also of the later things which will occur, there will be for them no remembrance among those who will come later still.

of Paul's tutelage, I would like to suggest to the reader that the modern church similarly needs a strong dose of history *for its instruction*. Biblical history and, even church history, supplies a vast array of needed warnings for all who proudly think they stand. It is for this reason that we will begin with a lesson from history that will enable us to look carefully in the mirror of our own human frailty. The events that we will consider came at a time in history that was characterized by great joy and celebration in the 16th century - *the time of Pope Leo X and Johann Tetzel.*

Some may be skeptical about the thought of this period being a time of joy and celebration. For many, yes it was indeed. When Protestants reflect on the history of Tetzel and the sale of indulgences, they tend to focus on the dark theological cloud which hovered over such an evil practice. This is understandable, especially when we look upon the past with sound theological hindsight, but we should not miss the broader lessons supplied by this period. If we could set aside such hindsight and join the ranks and mindset of the common man in their day, we would find a somewhat different perspective. In reality, the people were filled with great joy and celebration at the sight of Tetzel as he proffered his religious wares. Phillip Schaff offers us a historical on-scene perspective of Tetzel's reception among the people:

"Tetzel traveled with great pomp and circumstance through Germany, and recommended with unscrupulous effrontery and declamatory eloquence the indulgences of the Pope to the large crowds who gathered from every quarter around him. He was received like a messenger from heaven. Priests, monks, and magistrates, men and women, old and young, marched in solemn procession with songs, flags, and candles, under the ringing of bells, to meet him and his fellow-monks, and followed them to the church; the papal Bull on a velvet cushion was placed on the high altar, a red cross with a silken banner bearing the papal arms was erected before it, and a large iron chest was put beneath the cross for the indulgence money. Such chests are still preserved in many places. The preachers, by daily sermons, hymns, and processions, urged the people, with extravagant laudations of the Pope's Bull, to purchase letters of indulgence for their own benefit, and at the same time played upon their sympathies for departed relatives and friends whom they might release from their sufferings in purgatory 'as soon as the penny tinkles in the box.'"[11]

The scene recreated by Schaff is rather alarming at many levels. The idea of the people celebrating the arrival of their religious oppressors strains credulity at one level; however, when we place ourselves within the mindset of the people, especially concerning their understanding of doctrine and ecclesiastical authority, we should not be so surprised by their celebratory spirit. Armed with nothing else but religious tradition and papal authority, the people did not have the requisite light needed to expose these religious charlatans. In the end, Tetzel was vigorously heralded because the Pope, the most celebrated person in the Roman Catholic world, offered the hope of forgiveness and redemption to the people. Schaff is quite clear when making a connection between Tetzel and the Pope:

> "...the papal Bull on a velvet cushion was placed on the high altar, *a red cross with a silken banner bearing the papal arms was erected before it...*" [12]

It is important to note that Tetzel was received with great fanfare and celebration because he represented to the people the hope of forgiveness by the presumed power and authority of the Pope. Moreover, Schaff's mention of the *Papal banner bearing the Papal*

---

[11] Schaff, P., & Schaff, D. S. *Vol. 7: History of the Christian church* (New York: Charles Scribner's Sons, 1910), 153.

[12] Ibid.

coat of arms is of greater import than the modern mind might grasp. In fact, any mention of a *coat of arms* brings to bear the vast subject of *heraldry* – the ancient art and science of conveying a person's identity, ranking, or pedigree by symbols placed on a coat of arms.[13] The enormity of the subject of heraldry far exceeds the focus of our study, however, in European cultures (especially ancient Europe) the *heraldry* conveyed through a coat of arms would be seen as more than mere artistry. Instead, it was a very precise and known language among the people. Such was the case with Tetzel's banner adorned with the papal coat of arms for Leo X. When we decipher the symbols of this banner, we see a remarkable conveyance of unquestioned authority:

1. The Papal Tiara: At the top of the coat of arms was the Papal tiara, or triple crown, which consisted of three layers most likely signifying the pope's threefold authority. This signification of authority is reflected in the traditional expression of papal coronation: *"Receive the tiara adorned with three crowns, and know that thou art father of princes and kings, ruler of the world, vicar on earth of our Saviour Jesus*

---

[13] William Craigie, James Murray, John Simpson, eds., *Oxford English Dictionary Electronic* (Oxford: Oxford University Press), Heraldry: "The art or science of a herald; now, esp. the art or science of blazoning armorial bearings and of settling the right of persons to bear arms or certain bearings; in connexion with which it deals with the tracing and recording of pedigrees, and deciding of questions of precedence."

Christ, to whom is honour and glory for ever and ever."[14] By this symbolism alone, the pope was seen as having headship, not only over the church, but over all princes, kings, and the entire world itself. In the minds of the people, the triple-crown was a powerful symbol of the pope's unquestionable authority over all things, spiritual and secular.

2. The Papal Shield: Just below the Papal tiara stood the Papal shield. The shield typically communicated the pedigree and status of the individual it represented.[15] In the case of Pope Leo X, his shield bore 5 red balls and one blue one in the center, at the top of the shield. To the untrained eye, it signifies nothing more than an interesting decoration, but in the 16th century, it conveyed the unmistakable identity of the powerful Medici family. The extent of their power and influence as a political and banking family is somewhat difficult to grasp, but by the 15th century the Medici bank was the largest in Europe. As a family they were wealthy, well connected, and revered among the people. By this symbol alone, Pope Leo X was seen as much more than an average pope. He was a man who had vast connections as a member of one of Europe's most powerful and wealthy families.

3. The Two Keys of the Kingdom: Layered behind the Papal shield lay two keys in an opposing position.[16] These keys symbolized the

---

[14] Loraine Boettner, Roman Catholicism (Phillipsburg: The Presbyterian and Reformed Publishing Company, 1962), 127.

[15] Arthur Charles Fox-Davies, *A Complete Guide to Heraldry* (The Gutenburg Press, 2012), 61.

[16] "The symbolism of the keys is brought out in an ingenious and interpretative fashion by heraldic art. One of the keys is of gold (or), the other of silver (argent). The golden key, which points upwards on the dexter side, signifies the power that extends even to Heaven. The silver key, which must point up to the sinister side, symbolizes the power over all the faithful on earth. The two are often linked by a cordon Gules as a sign of the union of the two powers. The handles are turned downwards, for they are in the hand of the Pope, Christ's lieutenant on earth. The wards point upwards, for the power of binding and loosing engages Heaven itself." Bruno Bernhard Heim, Heraldry in the Catholic Church: Its Origin, Customs and Laws (Van Duren: 1978), 54.

Pope's power over the souls of men such that "...he can release whatever souls he pleases from further suffering [in Purgatory] and those whom he refuses to release are continued in their suffering, the decisions he makes on earth being ratified in heaven."[17] This third symbol stood as an ominous reminder to the people that the fate of their own souls, as well as the souls of loved ones in Purgatory, depended entirely on the one who was considered to be *vicar of Jesus Christ on earth.*

4. The Fleur-de-lis: The Papal tiara and the centered, blue Medici ball were both adorned with the familiar *fleur-de-lis* – a decorative yellow lily comprised of three large petals: one pointing to the left, one to the right, and one pointing upward. The history of this symbolism is quite extensive, beyond the realm of our need in this point, however the *fleur-de-lis* typically conveyed the idea of authority, whether political, dynastic, monarchial, or religious.[18] In the case of Leo X, all such notions of *authority* were implied in view of his title as *father of princes and kings, ruler of the world, vicar on earth of our Saviour Jesus Christ.*

Tetzel's *heraldic* procession of Papal authority sent an awe-inspiring message to the people, persuading them to receive their religious overlords with great celebration. The powerful imagery of Pope Leo's coat of arms provided the people with a form of hope for deliverance from sin and punishment. Such a hope as this wasn't just the mindset of a few, it had become the universal mindset of those under papal rule due to the near absence of critical voices. However, Pope Leo's banner of authority, replete with its religious symbolism, was a complete sham due to his utter abandonment of the Gospel of Jesus Christ. The story of Tetzel and his sale of indulgences is indeed remarkable, but I would submit to the reader that the deeper lesson of history is the one

---

[17] Boettner, <u>Roman Catholicism</u>, 128.

[18] Thomas Woodcock and John Martin Robinson, <u>The Oxford Guide to Heraldry</u>, (Oxford: Oxford University Press, 1988), 65.

which considers the gradual downgrade which led to the monstrosities of Pope Leo X. It isn't Satan's practice to announce his presence as he seeks to infiltrate and corrupt the church, instead, he presents himself as an angel of light with the heraldry of a *faux* authority. Should we ignore such lessons from history, we run the risk of falling into the Devil's most ancient trap. From the very beginning, Satan has relied on the tactic of incremental deception in order to lead others astray. A careful examination of his temptation of the woman in the garden, in Genesis 3, reveals the longstanding battle strategy of our enemy. Rather than issuing an overt demand that Adam and his wife engage in open rebellion against the Lord, the Serpent of old tempted the woman through a sequence of covert deceptions, the details of which are quite stunning when studied carefully. When the Apostle Paul confronted the Corinthians' dangerous flirtations with heresy, he reminded them of Satan's historic tactics of deception:

> 2 Corinthians 11:2–4: 2 For I am jealous for you with a godly jealousy; for I betrothed you to one husband, so that to Christ I might present you as a pure virgin. 3 But I am afraid that, as the serpent deceived Eve by his craftiness, your minds will be led astray from the simplicity and purity of devotion to Christ. 4 For if one comes and preaches another Jesus whom we have not preached, or you receive a different spirit which you have not received, or a different gospel which you have not accepted, you bear this beautifully.

When we recall Paul's ministry in Corinth from the beginning, it is rather striking to consider how this church was birthed with a sound beginning, but then descended into a state of remarkable corruption as evidenced by Paul's corrective letters to the church. Their descent into error was not immediate, but incremental. Over time, Satan had managed to shift their reverence and esteem for

God's word to that of another Gospel that was no Gospel at all.[19] It is this very concept of *incipient error and compromise* that has repeatedly raised its ugly head throughout the annals of human history. Such error often sprouts from the seed of an *ungodly fear* which scorns God's sovereignty and justice, while exalting man-made religion. Bunyan well summarized this matter in, *A Treatise of the Fear of God*:

> "...ungodly fear of God is that which will put men upon adding to the revealed will of God their own inventions, and their own performances of them, as a means to pacify the anger of God...it was this fear that put the Pharisees upon inventing so many traditions, as the washing of cups, and beds, and tables...; How it racked and tortured the Papists for hundreds of years together...for their penances, as creeping to the cross, going barefoot on pilgrimage, whipping themselves, wearing of sackcloth, saying so many Pater-nosters, so many Ave-marias, making so many confessions to the priest, giving so much money for pardons, and abundances of other the like..."[20]

When we stand back and consider the broader history which led to Pope Leo X, and his blasphemous sale of indulgences, we must remember that his doctrinal monstrosities were not created overnight. The apostasy of his day was first conceived many centuries prior. What we must recall is the fact that from the time of Constantine to the eve of the Reformation, the visible church endured a slow, incremental decay. Though the church in her earliest days reverenced Christ and His authority, this eventually gave way to a reverence for man-centered religion. Justo Gonzalez offers an excellent summary of these earliest corruptions in the church, in his book, *The Story of Christianity*:

---

[19] 2 Corinthians 11:4.

[20] John Bunyan, *A Treatise of the Fear of God* (Kindle Edition) in *Works of John Bunyan — Complete*, (Locations 19486-19487).

Clergy Veneration: "After Constantine's conversion, Christian worship began to be influenced by imperial protocol. Incense, which was used as a sign of respect for the emperor, began appearing in Christian churches. Officiating ministers, who until then had worn everyday clothes, began dressing more luxurious garments. Likewise, a number of gestures indicating respect, which were normally made before the emperor, now became part of Christian worship..."[21]

The Veneration of Saints & Relics: "...in the second century, it had become customary to commemorate the anniversary of a martyr's death by celebrating communion where the martyr had been buried. Now (in Constantine's time) churches were built in many of those places. Eventually, some came to think that worship was particularly valid if it was celebrated in one of those holy places, where the relics of a martyr were present. In consequence, some began to unearth the buried bodies of martyrs in order to place them-or part of them-under the altar of one of the many churches that were being built. Others began claiming revelations of martyrs who had not been known, or who had been almost forgotten...eventually, the relics of saints and of New Testament times were said to have miraculous powers. Empress Helena, the mother of Constantine, gave special impetus to this entire development when, in a pilgrimage to the Holy Land, she thought she had discovered the very cross of Christ. Soon this cross was said to have miraculous powers, and pieces of wood claiming to come from it were found all over the Empire.[22]

The Veneration of Religious Trends: "While these developments were taking place, many leaders of the church viewed them with disfavor, and tried to prevent superstitious extremes. Thus, a common theme of preaching was that it was not necessary to go to the Holy Land in order to be a good Christian, and that the respect due to the

---

[21] Justo L. Gonzalez, The Story of Christianity Vol I (San Francisco: Harper & Row, Publishers, 1984), 125.

[22] Ibid.

martyrs should not be exaggerated. But such preaching was unequal to the task, for people were flocking into the church in such numbers that there was little time to prepare them for baptism, and even less to guide them in Christian life once they had been baptized."[23]

While there is nothing inherently wrong with the impulse of *celebrating the piety* of saints and martyrs of yesteryear, the reality is that such practices tend to yield a shift, from reverence for Christ to a reverence for man and his religious inventions. As we look into the mirror and see our own human frailty, we find a very strong and idolatrous inclination to exalt various people and things above the Lord Jesus Christ. Human flesh requires no training or practice in order to achieve this end. It is all quite a part of our human frailty, and we must face this enemy in order to oppose it at every front. In the end, we must confess and realize this crucial fact: *in a wicked and fallen world, popularity and acclaim isn't necessarily a good thing.*[24] Pope Leo X and Johann Tetzel were the celebrated men of their day, but this stands as a testament to the darkness of the time. From the very beginning, Satan's agenda has remained essentially the same. His goal is to lead men astray by directing them away from truth, and this he does by presenting his own substitutes for the Lord's ultimate authority. Loraine Boettner says it well in his prescient summary of the church's downgrade during this time:

> "...we need only read church history to discover that when another source of authority is placed alongside Scripture as of equal importance, Scripture eventually becomes relegated to the background...If that other source be reason, we get rationalism. If it be emotion, we get mysticism. And if it be tradition, we get ecclesiastical

---

[23] Ibid., 126.
[24] 1 John 5:19.

dictation or clericalism. In each case the Bible, while still given lip service, is effectually superseded."[25]

Biblical history and church history stand together as a significant warning to the modern church, and we need such warnings. The papal banners of yesteryear now seem like ancient history and therefore we may be tempted to think that the modern era is free from the signs and symbols of such false authority. However, I would suggest to the reader that modern Evangelicalism has its own form of heraldic banners and symbols, all of which convey various messages of doctrine and authority. And while Evangelicalism claims no formal office of popedom, it does border on having its own form of Evangelical papalism through the exaltation of individuals who are esteemed far above their true station. For example, for many today a little-known Bible teacher *is just a Bible teacher*; but a reputable scholar who is well decorated with an assortment of degrees is often assumed to be *so much more than a mere Bible teacher*. Thus, the presumption often made is that academic achievement and acclaim is a form of doctrinal coronation, and the possessor of such degrees is thereby affirmed as a sound teacher *by default*. Though this form of thinking is common in society, Scripture nowhere advances such thinking. The Jewish rulers and elders of the 1st century certainly thought this way, and it is for this reason that they were astonished by the display of wisdom and power manifested by two simple fishermen, Peter and John:

> Acts 4:13: Now as they observed the confidence of Peter and John, and understood that they were uneducated and untrained men, they were marveling, and began to recognize them as having been with Jesus.

---

[25] Boettner, <u>Roman Catholicism</u>, 89.

Clearly, higher education is not inherently a bad thing; but neither is it a guarantee of genuine wisdom or piety. As well, if a teacher in the modern day is a pastor of a megachurch; is well connected with reputable parachurch organizations; is a frequent conference speaker; or is reputed to be a highly acclaimed author, then similar assumptions of piety and orthodoxy are often made simply on the basis of the individual's visibility and popularity. Moreover, those whose published titles make the New York Times' bestseller list are crowned with a *veritable fleur-de-lis* triple-crown in the eyes of many. Though modern-day Evangelicalism hasn't the sophisticated language like the heraldry of yesteryear, it certainly has its own signs and symbols of piety, authority, and orthodoxy that are readily *reverenced* by the masses, with little or no scrutiny. Those who rely on such modern-day heraldry, whether prominent teachers or their followers, are propagating a dangerous trend in the church. Such thinking derogates Christ while placing the student of Scripture in the dangerous place of *passive learning,* where critical analysis is replaced with thoughtless acceptance of what is being said. In such a case as this, the individual who is blinded by the limelight of their celebrated teacher relaxes his grip on the priority of *Sola Scriptura.* Also, by making the celebrated teacher an idol, he mutilates the priority of *Solus Christus.* It is for this reason that the modern day dangers of *celebritism* warrant serious attention, not just for the students of the word, but also for those who presume to serve as teachers of the word.[26] In the end, an individual's dignity, integrity, piety, and veracity cannot be assessed by the aforementioned heraldic standards of the modern day. Alternately, one must never assume that the possession of academic degrees, popularity, or published books automatically indicates *impiety or error.* In the end, the tests for any teacher

---

[26] James 3:1: LET not many of you become teachers, my brethren, knowing that as such we shall incur a stricter judgment.

must be established by much higher standards: the standards of God's word *and nothing else.*

Finally, with these lessons from history before us, let us conclude with a familiar picture from John Bunyan's classic book, *Pilgrim's Progress*, a book that he wrote while imprisoned for preaching the Gospel. In his allegory, Bunyan presents us with the characters, Christian and Hopeful, who had become weary of their travels along the narrow pathway which leads to the Celestial City (Heaven). In their weariness and weakness, their attention was drawn to a green meadow called By-path Meadow which ran alongside the narrow pathway in which they were travelling. This By-path Meadow, which was just off to their left, *appeared* to have an easier terrain for weary travelers. After some discussion about the matter, they climbed over a *stile* (*a crossing*) onto By-path Meadow. To their surprise and disappointment, Christian and Hopeful found that this alternate course was not easier at all, instead, it was nothing more than a dangerous divergence which left them lost, weary, and fearful. Eventually they were captured and enslaved by Giant Despair and cast into Doubting Castle. After having suffered greatly in the giant's castle for a while, they were able to escape using the key of Promise. The depth and richness of Bunyan's allegory exceeds our focus here, but what happens next underscores the lesson of this chapter. Upon their return to the narrow way over the stile, they resolved to erect a *pillar* with a message of warning to other pilgrims concerning the dangers of straying from the narrow pathway of Christ:

> "Now, when they were gone over the stile, they began to contrive with themselves what they should do at that stile, to prevent those that shall come after from falling into the hands of Giant Despair. So they consented to erect there a pillar, and to engrave upon the side thereof this sentence: "Over this stile is the way to Doubting Castle, which is

kept by Giant Despair, who despiseth the King of the Celestial country, and seeks to destroy his holy pilgrims." *Many, therefore, that followed after, read what was written, and escaped the danger.*[27]

Bunyan's allegory strongly magnifies the dangers of straying to the left or to the right of God's narrow pathway.[28] As well, he reminds us of the importance of the lessons of history. In his allegory, only those who observed and obeyed the warnings left on the *pillar* were able to escape the danger of By-path Meadow. Such imagery reminds us of our need to learn well from the lessons of history, *lest we think we stand and resultantly fall into the repeated sins of history.*

---

[27] John Bunyan, *The Pilgrim's Progress: From this world to that which is to come,* (Oak Harbor, WA: Logos Research Systems, Inc., 1995).
[28] Joshua 1:7-8.

MY
BANNER
IS
CHRIST

~ CHAPTER II ~

BEING SUBJECT

IN THE

FEAR OF CHRIST

In the previous chapter we considered the curious joy and willingness of many to receive Tetzel and his indulgences. We also considered the ominous signs and symbols of authority which led the people to believe that the Pope could bring them genuine hope and reconciliation. The heraldry of Pope Leo X delivered a fearful display of unquestioned authority, and the people were eager to bow, reverently, to such authority. Altogether, such a scene of *joy and reverence* reveals Satan's grim sense of irony and mockery, after all, the church was never called to give such *joyful reverence* to anyone but the Lord Himself:

> Psalm 2:11–12: 11 Worship the LORD with reverence, And rejoice with trembling. 12 Do homage to the Son, lest He become angry, and you perish in the way, For His wrath may soon be kindled. How blessed are all who take refuge in Him!

Satan is a master at turning truth on its head in the minds of those whom he deceives. True worship has always consisted of rendering a *joyful reverence* to the Lord, and it is for this reason that Devil has always sought to mutilate such a reality. John Calvin helps us to consider the importance of this matter:

> "...no man can rightly handle the doctrine of godliness, unless the fear of God reign and bear the chief sway in him."[29]

When we examine some of the principal expressions of worship in the early church, we find that believers were strongly invested in the beauty and simplicity of Psalm 2: *joyful reverence*. For example, when Luke described the Jerusalem church's loving devotion to Christ in Acts 2:42-47, he indicated that they *kept feeling a sense of awe (phobos - fear),*[30] with *exceeding joy (agalliasei).*[31] These are

---

[29] John Calvin, *Calvin's Commentary - Acts* (Albany, OR: Ages Software, 1995).
[30] Acts 2:43.

not contradictory affections, but instead they harmonize as the Spirit's genuine fruit within a believer. Such joyful reverence for God is crucial, however, if such adoration is given to men, then Satan's malicious goals have been fulfilled. In every age, the absence of godly fear has helped to create the fertile soils out of which man-centered religion has flourished. Whenever the church succumbs to a reverence and adoration of mere men, she enters into the darkness of idolatry and spiritual mayhem. Such a downgrade is most often evidenced by an irreverence for the Scriptures, as John Bunyan argues:

> "'Heaven and earth,' saith Christ, 'shall pass away, but my words shall not pass away' (Matt 24:35)...*This, therefore, calleth upon God's people to stand more in fear of the Word of God than of all the terrors of the world.* There wanteth even in the hearts of God's people a greater reverence of the Word of God than to this day appeareth among us, and this let me say, that *want of reverence of the Word is the ground of all disorders that are in the heart, life, conversation, and in Christian communion.* Besides, the want of reverence of the Word layeth men open to the fearful displeasure of God—'Whoso despiseth the word shall be destroyed; but he that feareth the commandment shall be rewarded' (Prov 13:13)."[32] [italics mine]

I would submit to the reader that Bunyan's warning to the church is much needed in the modern day. If we are to give serious consideration to the priorities of *Solus Christus* and *Sola Scriptura*, then we must see to it that our devotion to Him remains uncorrupted by the fear or exaltation of anything other than Christ. Any church of any generation that has been drawn away from the priority of paying homage to Christ and His authority *alone* is a church that is in great danger. Bunyan is right when he

---

[31] Acts 2:46.

[32] Bunyan, *A Treatise of the Fear of God.*

reminds us that the fear of God is an important antidote against all disorders that arise when we surrender to false authorities. Sadly, centuries of weak and imbalanced preaching has made the notion of fearing God the object of suspicion and disdain. Even in the preaching of the Gospel, much of modern Evangelicalism has invented a kind of shallow, *irreverent faith*[33] as a substitute for genuine faith which sees God for who He truly is. Clearly, *irreverence* cannot be reconciled with *genuine faith and worship.* The sinner who comprehends that God *is*[34] and that He alone has the *awesome power and authority to forgive sin*[35] will *do homage to the Son.*[36] These truths bring back to life the Gospel realities that have been buried for decades by feckless preaching. Those who have been tutored under the direction of such shallow preaching typically become steeped in an abundance of doctrinal confusion. In the modern day, many churches are eager to advertise themselves as being casual, culturally relevant, and musically trendy, yet, how many of these same churches would be willing to place on their service advertisements this prescription for the church for all ages:

Ephesians 5:21: and be subject to one another *in the fear of Christ.* [italics mine]

---

[33] More will be said about the relationship between the fear of God and the Gospel in Appendix I of this book. In that section we will look more closely at John's description of *the eternal gospel* in his Apocalypse: Revelation 14:6–7: 6 And I saw another angel flying in midheaven, having an eternal gospel to preach to those who live on the earth, and to every nation and tribe and tongue and people; 7 and he said with a loud voice, "Fear God, and give Him glory, because the hour of His judgment has come; and worship Him who made the heaven and the earth and sea and springs of waters." As mentioned in the introduction, genuine faith will yield the fruit of trust, love, adoration, and godly reverence.

[34] Hebrews 11:6.

[35] Psalm 130:4.

[36] Psalm 2:12.

Many pulpits today will eagerly broadcast messages on love and joy; yet, fewer still would dare touch the subject of *fearing Christ*.[37] This is because the subject of fearing God has been dangerously transformed into an unwelcome stranger to the modern church. Many see the word *fear* and simply assume that this term necessarily denotes a loveless, joyless dread. However, such thinking runs contrary to Scripture. In the case of Ephesians 5:21, it is important to note that this description of pious living is indelibly linked to the believer's love for God. In the beginning of the fifth chapter of Ephesians, Paul issued two foundational injunctions: *"be imitators of God as beloved children"* and *"walk in love* just as Christ also loved you and gave Himself up for us." By itself, this conjoined premise establishes a unified foundation of love: God's love for His children and our response of love for God. What Paul then develops throughout the fifth chapter is a call to holy living as an expression of such love. Amidst this developed thought, Paul issued the command to *be filled with the Holy Spirit (v. 18)* followed by a series of descriptions of what a Spirit-filled life looks like in the context of the church: *"speaking to one another in psalms and hymns and spiritual songs, singing and making melody with your heart to the Lord" (v. 19); "always giving thanks for all things in the name of our Lord Jesus Christ to God, even the Father (20); and "being subject to one another in the fear of Christ" (21).* From the beginning of the fifth chapter to the end, Paul shows us the multiple facets and expressions of what a Christ-centered love

---

[37] Calvin surmised that some manuscripts contain *phobō theou* as the result of scribal edits: "Some Greek manuscripts read, "the fear of God." The change may have been introduced by some person, who thought that the other phrase, the fear of Christ, though by far the most appropriate, sounded a little harsh." Calvin, *Calvin's Commentaries: Eph 5:21.*

looks like.[38] Thus, all of the expressions of piety in Ephesians 5 are manifestations of a *walk of love* that is led by the Spirit and is the fruit of God's love for His children. It is for this reason that Paul's mention of fear, in verse 21 (*in the fear of Christ*), points to a loving, godly fear rather than an ungodly fear. Such a godly fear must not be confused with those who fearfully and disdainfully flee from the Lord out of their enmity with Him[39] and pending judgment from Him.[40] Instead, this is a fear which is an expression of love, joy, and worship as that which is given to the Son in view of His matchless worth (Psalm 2:11-12). This godly affection is, at its heart, a *filial fear* which draws us closer to our heavenly Father as his children, or as Bunyan rightly says:

"...it is that Spirit of grace that is the author, animator, and maintainer of our filial fear, or of that fear that is son-like, and that subjecteth the elect unto God, his word, and ways; unto him, his word, and ways, as a Father."[41]

Moreover, such filial fear turns the timid and weak soldier into a fearless warrior: a central theme developed within the sixth chapter of Ephesians. Flavel highlights this powerful truth regarding *filial fear*, reminding us of our need to be bold servants and soldiers for Christ:

---

[38] When we include Paul's expansive teaching on the subject of love elsewhere, we must remember that the first fruit of the Spirit is love (Galatians 5:22), and that without such love we are nothing (1 Corinthians 13:2). Thus, all of the expressions of piety in Ephesians 5 are manifestations of a walk of love that is led by the Spirit. Please see Appendix II for an expanded treatment of this subject.

[39] Revelation 6:12-17.

[40] More will be said about John's contrast between love and ungodly fear (1 John 4:17-18) in Appendix I.

[41] Bunyan, *A Treatise of the Fear of God.*

"If a man do really look to God in a day of trouble and fear as to the Lord of hosts, i.e. one that governs all the creatures, and all their actions; at whose beck and command all the armies of heaven and earth are, and then can rely upon the care and love of this God, as a child in danger of trouble reposes on, and commits him-self with greater confidence to the care and protection of his father: O what peace, what rest, must necessarily follow upon this! Who would be afraid to pass through the midst of armed troops and regiments, whilst he knows that the general of the army is his own father? The more power this filial fear of God obtains in our hearts, the less will you dread the power of the creature."[42]

Sadly, what was common knowledge among the Puritan pulpits of yesteryear has become an unwanted stranger in the present day. The modern church's timidity concerning the subject of fearing God poses no small problem. Modern preachers who make it their business to airbrush such truths out of their sermons are raising up a generation of people who feel a license to approach the Scriptures on the basis of their own thoughts, preferences, and affections. Whenever preachers emphasize a limited spectrum of God's attributes *according to their own preferences*, they create an idolatrous monster of which they become an officiating priest. Such obfuscations of truth not only pose a danger to believers, but it also assaults the Gospel and the church's witness to the world. In the end, a god of wrath and *no mercy* is just as much a false deity as is its reverse: a god of mercy and *no wrath*. However, when preachers follow the apostolic example of *proclaiming the whole counsel of God*[13] they avoid idolatrous extremes and are therefore free from the bloodguilt of lying to others about the true nature and will of God. It is in this latter sphere of preaching ministry that

---

[42] Flavel, A Practical Treatise of Fear, 244.

[13] Acts 20:26–27: 26 Wherefore I testify unto you this day, that I am pure from the blood of all men. 27 For I shrank not from declaring unto you the whole counsel of God. [ASV]

the biblical realities of Godly fear should flourish in faithful pulpits.

Despite its modern unpopularity, the doctrine of *fearing God* is as ancient as the eternal Gospel itself: "And I saw another angel flying in midheaven, having an *eternal gospel* to preach to those who live on the earth, and to every nation and tribe and tongue and people; and he said with a loud voice, '*Fear God*, and give Him glory, because the hour of His judgment has come; and worship Him who made the heaven and the earth and sea and springs of waters...'" (Revelation 14:6–7, italics mine). Such fear is a tender and loving work of grace which draws God's children closer to Him, "...I will put the fear of Me in their hearts so that they will not turn away from Me" (Jeremiah 32:40). This godly fear is a cure for our spiritual double-mindedness: "Teach me Thy way, O LORD; I will walk in Thy truth. Unite my heart to fear Your name" (Psalm 86:11) and it is central to genuine wisdom, for without it we become utter fools, for "the fear of the Lord is the beginning of wisdom" (Psalm 111:10). Such fear gives us a holy hatred for evil, "The fear of the Lord is to hate evil" (Proverbs 8:13) and it helps us to see that God's forgiveness of the sinner is truly *awesome*,[44] "...there is forgiveness with Thee, that Thou mayest be feared" (Psalm 130:4). Without godly reverence we fall short of the heavenly standard of true worship, "...Give praise to our God, all you His bond-servants, *you who fear Him*, the small and the great." (Revelation 19:5, italics mine). Overall, as stated earlier, those who fear God as He deserves are entrusted with His banner of truth, "Thou hast given a banner to those who fear Thee, that it may be displayed because of the truth. [Selah]" (Psalm 60:4). Many will

---

[44] Our modern culture has sadly degraded the word *awesome* to a slang equivalent of the term "cool," however, in this book this biblical word is used in its historic, denotative sense of that which inspires *awe* or *fear* in an individual.

flock to a deity that is portrayed as having a universal love, mercy, and grace for all without exception, but fewer still will bow the knee to the One who is worthy of the creature's unmitigated awe, reverence, and obedience. Understanding this principle, Satan has consistently promoted the idol of a *fearless deity* in whom sinners are called to place a kind of *irreverent faith*.[45] All of this the Devil promotes in place of the Scriptural truth regarding the One to whom godly fear *is due*:

> Jeremiah 10:6–7: 6 There is none like Thee, O LORD; Thou art great, and great is Thy name in might. 7 Who would not fear Thee, O King of the nations? Indeed it is Thy due! For among all the wise men of the nations, And in all their kingdoms, There is none like Thee.

For those who would dismiss the doctrine of godly fear as that which only belongs to the Old Covenant, they should consider that heavenly refrain found in John's Apocalypse:

> Revelation 15:4 "Who will not fear, O Lord, and glorify Thy name? For Thou alone art holy; For ALL THE NATIONS WILL COME AND WORSHIP BEFORE THEE, For Thy righteous acts have been revealed."

Believers in every generation desperately need the penetrating and fearful query of Jeremiah 10 and Revelation 15: *who will not fear and glorify His name?* Such a needed call to reverential worship

---

[45] The use of the expression *irreverent faith* here and throughout this book points to the notion of a false faith which leads to irreverence and rebellion. True faith consists of a belief and trust that *God is* (Hebrews 11:6); is focused on the person and work of Jesus Christ (Acts 16:31); and yields the fruit of love, adoration, worship, and godly fear for Him as Lord and Savior (Revelation 14:6-7). It should be noted, however, that men and demons can have a form of faith which causes them to tremble at the sight of God (James 2:19), but such faith is shallow and devoid of true trust, love, adoration, and godly reverence.

should remind us that the Lord shares His glory with no one[46] and therefore He calls us to fear and glorify Him *alone*. When the church heralds the banner of Christ's glory, she demonstrates her loving, joyful, and reverent fidelity to her Bridegroom.[47] However, when the church falters at this, she reveals herself to be Hosea's Gomer.

In all of this, I wish to echo Bunyan's expressed concern that "want of reverence of the Word is the ground of all disorders that are in the heart, life, conversation, and in Christian communion." By underscoring his sentiment, I must admit that there is much more to be said about the importance of godly, Christian affections than just fear itself. Having already written other works focusing on the foremost affection of love, I will here offer a more narrow examination of the Christian's need for godly fear as well as the danger of *irreverence: the absence of the fear of Christ.* In order to expand upon this important subject, we will first look at the one who instructed us to serve one another in the fear of Christ: the Apostle Paul.

Whenever we look at Paul's life, it seems difficult to comprehend the extent of his temptations and trials, especially in light of his unique calling. Christ promised that Paul would have to face men of great prominence, *even kings*, while enduring opposition for the sake of the Gospel: "But the Lord said to him, 'Go, for he is a

---

[46] "...you shall not worship any other god, for the LORD, whose name is Jealous, is a jealous God" (Exodus 34:14).

[47] In addition to our analysis of Paul's development of the subjects of love and reverence in Ephesians 5, we should also note the wife's imitation of the church's reverent relationship with Christ (Ephesians 5:20). In the concluding verse of Ephesians 5 (v. 33), Paul enjoins wives to reverence [*phobētai*] their husbands in the pattern of the church's reverence for her Head, Christ: Eph 5:33 Nevertheless let every one of you in particular so love his wife even as himself; and the wife see that she reverence [*phobētai* – *lit. fear*] her husband. [AV]

chosen instrument of Mine, to bear My name before the Gentiles and kings and the sons of Israel; for I will show him how much he must suffer for My name's sake'" (Acts 9:15–16). Here is a man who bore the brandmarks of Jesus,[48] having been imprisoned, beaten and left for dead, lashed thirty-nine times, nearly stoned to death, having faced multiple dangers including false brethren and shipwreck at sea.[49] In some sense, Paul seems to be a stranger to fear such that, when writing from prison, he exhorted the Philippians to rejoice[50] and called upon Timothy to join him in "suffering for the Gospel."[51] Yet, we must exercise caution amidst all this talk about the Apostle Paul's boldness in Christ, lest we find ourselves exalting a mere man and burning incense in his memory. After all, when Paul ministered the word in Corinth he was met with significant resistance from a number of Jews and the effect this had on him is quite instructive:

Acts 18:9: And the Lord said to Paul in the night by a vision, "Do not be afraid any longer, but go on speaking and do not be silent;"

We must not miss the realities of what is revealed in this vision. Paul had to be commanded by the Lord *to cease from fearing men and to resist the temptation of being silent*. By implication, both of these commands show that Paul had been struggling with fear in view of the opposition he was receiving in Corinth, and he was thereby tempted to be silent for the sake of his own self-preservation. What this confirms for us is that Paul was a frail human just like the rest of us! It would be a catastrophic error on our part to miss these important details in Acts 18, falsely assuming that Paul never struggled with such temptations. The

---

[48] Galatians 6:17.

[49] 2 Corinthians 11:25-27.

[50] Philippians 3:1.

[51] 2 Timothy 1:8.

reality is that the true story of Paul *is not about Paul*. Rather, the story of Paul is about the One who graciously elected, redeemed, and powerfully sanctified his soul. In the end, who is this man named Paul? A frail man whose weakness magnified the power of Christ.[52] The Savior's instruction to Paul in Acts 18:9 strongly parallels his earlier warnings concerning the danger of fearing men:

> Matthew 10:24–26, 28, 31-33: 24 "A disciple is not above his teacher, nor a slave above his master. 25 "It is enough for the disciple that he become like his teacher, and the slave like his master. If they have called the head of the house Beelzebul, how much more will they malign the members of his household! 26 "***Therefore do not fear them***, for there is nothing concealed that will not be revealed, or hidden that will not be known... 28 "***Do not fear those*** who kill the body but are unable to kill the soul; but ***rather fear Him*** who is able to destroy both soul and body in hell...31 "***So do not fear***; you are more valuable than many sparrows. 32 "Therefore everyone who confesses Me before men, I will also confess him before My Father who is in heaven. 33 "But ***whoever denies Me*** before men, I will also deny him before My Father who is in heaven." [*bold, italics mind*]

Christ issued the warning about denying Him in view of a *fear inducing world of opposition to Christ and His disciples*. Clearly, His warnings are rooted in the reality of our human propensity towards fearing men rather than God. Should we ever think that we are above such warnings, we can be sure that we have entered into the sin of pride. Whether we fear the loss of reputation, popularity, property, public influence, or our very lives, all such fear is the pathway to rebellion and even apostasy. Yet, when we render fear to the One who deserves it, all of our heart-confusion

---

[52] 2 Corinthians 10:7-12.

and hypocrisy is supplanted with a *singleness of heart* toward God *alone.* As Bunyan rightly puts it:

"There flows from this godly fear of God 'singleness of heart' (Col 3:22). Singleness of heart both to God and man; singleness of heart, that is it which in another place is called sincerity and godly simplicity, and it is this, when a man doth a thing simply for the sake of him or of the law that commands it, without respect to this by-end, or that desire of praise or of vain-glory from others...when our obedience to God is done by us simply or alone for God's sake, for his Word's sake, without any regard to this or that by-end or reserve, 'not with eye-service, as men-pleasers, but in singleness of heart, fearing God.'"[53]

Paul's struggles with the fear of men and the temptation to remain silent in the face of his opponents were radically transformed by his desire to minister *in the fear of Christ.* Paul clearly became a man of distinct boldness after his momentary struggles in Corinth, and by this we are reminded that his mention of being subject *in the fear of Christ* was rooted in deep conviction. Throughout his ministry, the thought of fearfully shrinking back from declaring God's word became unthinkable. In his departing testimony before the elders at Ephesus, Paul expanded on this unbending commitment of his:

Acts 20:24–27: 24 "But I do not consider my life of any account as dear to myself, in order that I may finish my course, and the ministry which I received from the Lord Jesus, to testify solemnly of the gospel of the grace of God. 25 "And now, behold, I know that all of you, among whom I went about preaching the kingdom, will see my face no more. 26 "Therefore I testify to you this day, that I am innocent of the blood of all men. 27 "For I did not shrink from declaring to you the whole purpose of God."

---

[53] Bunyan, *A Treatise of the Fear of God.*

Before leaving the church at Ephesus, Paul reminded the church's elders of his Apostolic priority and example of *declaring the whole purpose*[54] *of God.* Thus, Paul was not a "soap-box preacher," picking and choosing the truths that he wanted to emphasize the most, or pressing teachings that he thought would appeal to the masses; instead, his presentation of God's word was as broad as the full spectrum of God's divine revelation to mankind. Paul ministered the gospel of the grace of God to the residents in Ephesus for three years, the results of which caused "no small disturbance concerning the Way,"[55] yet he continued "to testify solemnly of the gospel of the grace of God."[56] Paul clearly states that he was *innocent from the blood of all men* because he did not shrink back from declaring *the whole purpose of God.* As for this interesting expression, *innocent from the blood of all men*, it strongly resembles God's instruction to Ezekiel about faithful and unfaithful watchmen:

> Ezekiel 33:1–6: 1 AND the word of the LORD came to me saying, 2 "Son of man, speak to the sons of your people, and say to them, 'If I bring a sword upon a land, and the people of the land take one man from among them and make him their watchman; 3 and he sees the sword coming upon the land, and he blows on the trumpet and warns the people, 4 then he who hears the sound of the trumpet and does not take warning, and a sword comes and takes him away, his blood will be on his own head. 5 'He heard the sound of the trumpet, but did not take warning; his blood will be on himself. But had he taken warning, he would have delivered his life. 6 'But if the watchman sees the sword coming and does not blow the trumpet, and the people are not warned, and a sword comes and takes a person from them, he is taken away in his iniquity; but his blood I will require from the watchman's hand.'

---

[54] G. *Boulēn* – the volition, intention, counsel.

[55] Acts 19:23.

[56] Acts 20:24.

Paul understood what it meant to be a faithful watchman, while dreading the failure of those who flee like a hireling. The one who *shrinks back* from issuing Gospel warnings to others bears the bloodguilt of those who remain condemned. However, the watchman who warns the people bears no such guilt. Because Paul did not shrink back from declaring God's profitable word[57] he was able to say that he was innocent of such bloodguilt. As a faithful watchman, Paul's greatest concern wasn't the avoidance of controversy. Instead, his preaching ministry in Ephesus led to many confessing their sinful practices[58] and, as a result, the whole city was filled with rage over the divisive effects of the Gospel.[59] Yes, Paul's preaching of God's word sparked a riot in Ephesus, but at no time did he forsake his calling. A careful perusal of his entire ministry demonstrates that this was his normal practice *by God's grace.*

We must also consider Paul's dealings with men of prominence within the church. Up to this point, we have looked at the conflicts which Paul experienced from unbelievers who resisted the Gospel. Yet, how did Paul's subjection and servitude in the fear of Christ influence him in his ministry among God's people? Well, it had the same result of heralding Christ and His authority alone:

> Galatians 1:10: For am I now seeking the favor of men, or of God? Or am I striving to please men? *If I were still trying to please men, I would not be a bond-servant of Christ.* [italics mine]

Paul's love and reverence for Christ purged him of the wickedness of being a man-pleaser. His expressed disdain for such man-centeredness offers an important premise to his description of the

---

[57] Acts 20:20.
[58] Acts 19:18-19.
[59] Acts 19:17-30.

Galatian conflict in the second chapter. There, Paul indicated that he had to oppose Cephas to his face in view of an intolerable compromise of the Gospel:

> Galatians 2:11–14: 11 But when Cephas came to Antioch, I opposed him to his face, because he stood condemned. 12 For prior to the coming of certain men from James, he used to eat with the Gentiles; but when they came, he began to withdraw and hold himself aloof, fearing the party of the circumcision. 13 And the rest of the Jews joined him in hypocrisy, with the result that even Barnabas was carried away by their hypocrisy. 14 But when I saw that they were not straightforward about the truth of the gospel, I said to Cephas in the presence of all, "If you, being a Jew, live like the Gentiles and not like the Jews, how is it that you compel the Gentiles to live like Jews?"

Paul's actions clearly reveal his regard for the Gospel over and above that of highly esteemed men. Cephas capitulated to the pressures of a group of influential Judaizers, and such co-belligerence had spread to Barnabas and others. Despite such compromise, Paul's stand on the Gospel would not be changed for *God shows no partiality* among men (Galatians 2:6). Paul had to oppose Cephas to his face, "in the presence of all," in order to crush such Gospel-destroying influences. Had Paul shrunk back from such a public confrontation, the corruptions introduced through Cephas would have continued to plague the church. Calvin well advises us on the dangers of such compromise:

> "This shews us how cautiously we ought to guard against giving way to the opinions of men, lest an immoderate desire to please, or an undue dread of giving offense, should turn us aside from the right path. If this might happen to Peter, how much more easily may it happen to us, if we are not duly careful!"[60]

---

[60] Calvin, Calvin's Commentaries: *Galatians 2:12*.

It is interesting to note that the driving force behind Cephas' compromise was that of fear *[phoboumenos]*. We are not told if such fear came as the result of *an immoderate desire to please or an undue dread of giving offense,* however, the end result remains the same. The revered Judaizers planted their bad seeds, Cephas watered, and the weeds of error began spreading quickly. Cephas' momentary weakness reveals the grave danger of man-centered fear and it issues the important reminder concerning mankind's universal capacity to fear and pay homage to the creature rather than the Creator. Yet, no matter how celebrated or revered men may be in the world, we must resolve with Paul that *what they are makes no difference to us; God shows no partiality.*[61] Truth is truth, and it is never augmented nor diminished by mere men. In Christ, we are forbidden to fear or honor men above the Lord Himself. Paul's willingness to confront Cephas to his face would, no doubt, be seen by many in the modern day as an abusive, hateful response. Those who place men above the priority of revering and glorifying God will certainly think in this manner. But for Paul, who called God's people *to be subject to one another in the fear of Christ,* there was only one possible choice: to speak the truth in love and in reverence for Christ alone. By doing so, Paul modeled for us what a loving reverence for Christ and His word looks like:

1. The Priority of *Solus Christus*: When we hear teaching that is in error, our highest concern must be *vertical* (our relationship with the Lord) rather than *horizontal* (our relationship with men). Love and reverence for Christ will keep this priority in check, however, reverence for men will give birth to the monster of idolatry. God is truth, and therefore the believer should be most concerned about His glory whenever teachers fail to uphold the Scripture, no matter how popular

---

[61] Galatians 2:6.

they are. As our Savior Himself said, "He who has My commandments and keeps them is the one who loves Me..." (John 14:21).

2. The Priority of *Sola Scriptura*:[62] The Apostle Paul reminds us that love *does not rejoice in unrighteousness, but rejoices with the truth [1 Corinthians 13:6]*. Godly zeal for truth obliterates our indifference towards falsehood. Though some may consider it polite to ignore error where it is found, the Scripture calls this unloving. If we find someone who is in error, love compels us to speak the truth in love[63] as a ministry of mercy.[64] This is true friendship *in Christ* as opposed to the *deceitful kisses of an enemy* - Proverbs 27:6: *"Faithful are the wounds of a friend, But deceitful are the kisses of an enemy."*

Out of a loving reverence for Christ, Paul resisted the pressure to capitulate to Cephas and the Judaizers. What Paul did was not an act of cruelty, instead, he was serving Cephas and the church honorably. His experience and example stands as a pillar of warning to all who would chose a lesser pathway. Flavel strikes at the heart of the matter when he says:

"By the fear of the Lord men depart from evil (Proverbs 16:6), by the fear of man they run themselves into evil (Proverbs 29:5)."[65]

As the disciples of Christ, it is crucial that we remember just how easy it is to stray from the priority of reverencing and magnifying Christ *alone*. The plague of idolatry is a disease which infects every human heart. We are mindless fools to deny this, and we become our own worst enemy when we pridefully surmise that we are above the threat of such a contagion. Ultimately, this universal disease cannot be treated with superficial tonics or patches;

---

[62] Galatians 6:1.

[63] Ephesians 4:25.

[64] Jude 22-23.

[65] Flavel, A Practical Treatise of Fear, p. 252.

instead it must be rooted out and brutally slain on a daily basis, while remembering that only the Lord can *unite our hearts to fear His name*. Left to ourselves, our frail hearts are prone to herald things and people of inferior rank over and above the only One who deserves our singular love, devotion, adoration, worship, and fear. The wars of nations typically last only a handful of years, but the internal combat of the Christian is a lifelong struggle that only ends in death when we are translated into glory in the presence of our Lord and King. On his deathbed, Bunyan expressed some important thoughts about mankind's need for self-examination, reminding us all that, when the Lord issues His final judgment, the hearts of men will be fully disclosed:

> "When the sound of the trumpet shall be heard which shall summon the dead to appear before the tribunal of God, the righteous shall hasten out of their graves with joy to meet their Redeemer in the clouds; others shall call to the hills and mountains to fall upon them, to cover them from the sight of their Judge: let us therefore in time be posing [questioning] ourselves which of the two we shall be."[66]

If our fear of God is filial in nature, as an outpouring of love for our heavenly Father, then we have encouragement in the Spirit.[67] If our fear drives us to flee from God and His authority, then we should be gravely warned. It is imperative that we guard and watch over our hearts, remembering that we live in a world that is filled with countless stiles which lead away from the pathway of truth into the dangerous territory of *By-path Meadow*. For this reason, history, and especially Scripture itself, gives us important pillars of truth which offer strong warnings to pilgrims concerning the great dangers of straying from Christ and His absolute authority. Such

---

[66] John Bunyan, *Dying Sayings* (Kindle Edition) in *Works of John Bunyan — Complete*, (Location 5356).
[67] Romans 8:1-17.

warnings are a blessing to our soul when we heed them well. As the children of God, we must resolve to fight what the Apostle Paul called "the good fight" of faith.[68] One thing is for certain: we are not called to surrender to the enemy in such a battle. Such is the great and continual challenge that we all face. This is the central priority of all of God's children: to stand firm *in Christ alone* while forsaking all imposters and feigned substitutes of power or authority.

---

[68] 2 Timothy 4:7.

MY BANNER IS CHRIST

~ CHAPTER III ~

CELEBRITISM

AND THE WORSHIP

OF THE NEHUSHTAN

As those who are called to be subject to one another in the fear of Christ, we should remember the manner in which Paul modeled this for us all. When surrounded by men of renown who were in error, he did not shrink back from declaring the full counsel of God's word. Whenever faced with similar situations, we must recognize that taking a stand for truth may jeopardize some relationships, yet it honors the one relationship that matters most of all: our relationship with Jesus Christ. To herald God and His authority over men is not a dishonorable act, but an honorable one. As already noted, Paul's open contest with Cephas was not an expression of hateful aggression, instead it was an act of genuine love: *a love which does not rejoice in unrighteousness, but rejoices with the truth.* Whatever pressures we may face in this life, we must remember that we are called to herald the Savior and Head of the church and no one else. History reminds us that the diseases of man-centered celebritism and the fear of man have always flourished amidst those soils that have been depleted of a *joyful reverence for Christ.* Thus, wherever the fear of God wanes, the exaltation of men waxes hot. In the Gospels, we find that our Savior frequently exposed and rebuked such man-centeredness during His earthly ministry. At the time, 1st century Judaism had a very strong appearance of health and vibrance, but this was only an appearance. Beneath such a religious sheepskin lay the hidden beast of man-centered idolatry:

John 5:43–46: 43 "I have come in My Father's name, and you do not receive Me; if another comes in his own name, you will receive him. 44 "How can you believe, *when you receive glory from one another and you do not seek the glory that is from the one and only God?* 45 "Do not think that I will accuse you before the Father; the one who accuses you is Moses, *in whom you have set your hope.* 46 "For if you believed Moses, you would believe Me, for he wrote about Me." [*italics mine*]

Christ's indictment of the Jewish leadership of His day is both stunning and telling. In the above text, the Savior exposed the man-centeredness of his audience with this rebuke: *you receive glory [doxan] from one another and do not seek the glory [doxan] that is from the one and only God.* Christ's use of the word "glory" [*doxan*] reveals the fact that his audience was invested in the business of *glorifying* (i.e., praising or heralding) mere men. With such man-centered idolatry locked in place, these religious leaders had no room in their hearts for the Lord Himself. Moreover, Christ narrowed His rebuke by indicating that they were placing their hope in Moses, a mere messenger whose mission was to point to God's chosen Messiah – Jesus Christ. Though Moses was indeed a humble and godly man (Numbers 12:3, Hebrews 11:24-28), he was not to be the object of Israel's faith and adoration. Despite this obvious truth, many Jews were guilty of sinfully exalting mere men of prominence. John 5:43-46 reveals just one idolatrous event amidst countless transgressions in Israel's history. In the 7th century B.C., Hezekiah, king of Judah, brought about crucial reforms by removing the high places and sacred pillars, including one relic that invoked the memory of Moses:

> 2 Kings 18:1, 4: 1 Now it came about in the third year of Hoshea, the son of Elah king of Israel, that Hezekiah the son of Ahaz king of Judah became king...4 He removed the high places and broke down the sacred pillars and cut down the Asherah. *He also broke in pieces the bronze serpent that Moses had made, for until those days the sons of Israel burned incense to it; and it was called Nehushtan.* [italics mine]

The spiritual wickedness which Hezekiah faced in his day uncovers Israel's remarkable breadth of idolatry. The *Asherah* represented the Canaanite goddess who was known as *qaniyatu elima* – "progenitress/creatress of the gods."[69] From Israel's

---

[69] Archer & Waltke, *Theological Wordbook of the Old Testament.*

earliest days, the people of the nation were called upon to reject such pagan idolatry: "Watch yourself that you make no covenant with the inhabitants of the land (Amorite, Canaanite, Hittite, Perizzite, Hivite, Jebusite)...you are to tear down their altars and smash their sacred pillars and cut down their Asherim..." (Exodus 34:12–13). This is just one passage among many where we find the Lord warning the nation regarding the overt paganism of the Asherim. However, Israel's adoration of the Nehushtan represented a form of idolatry with a different history, seeing that the bronze serpent invoked the rich memory of God's dealings with Israel during her wilderness wanderings. In the book of Numbers, we learn about the origin and use of the bronze serpent:

> Numbers 21:8: Then the LORD said to Moses, "Make a fiery serpent, and set it on a standard; and it shall come about, that everyone who is bitten, when he looks at it, he shall live."

Moses carried out the Lord's command to make the bronze serpent and set it up on a standard and, as a result, all those who looked upon it lived in fulfillment of God's immutable promise (Numbers 21:8-9). Clearly, the object of Israel's faith and worship was to be the promise giver: the Lord Himself, not the brazen serpent, nor even Moses. The Lord had already revealed His jealous rage against all idolatry, whatever its form:

> Exodus 20:3–5: 3 "You shall have no other gods before Me. 4 "You shall not make for yourself an idol, or any likeness of what is in heaven above or on the earth beneath or in the water under the earth. 5 "You shall not worship them or serve them; for I, the LORD your God, am a jealous God, visiting the iniquity of the fathers on the children, on the third and the fourth generations of those who hate Me,

Whether men pay homage to the idols of their own making, or images of things in heaven, on the earth, or in the water; all such idolatrous creations constitute grave sin because they are offered as substitutes for the only One worthy of worship: the Lord God Almighty. It is for this reason that, despite the rich history of Moses and the Nehushtan, there could never be justification for the idolatrous actions taken by those in Hezekiah's and Christ's day. In each case, these individuals *worshiped the creature rather than the Creator.* However popular the worship of Moses' Nehushtan was among the Jews, Hezekiah removed Israel's idols because he "trusted in the Lord..." and "kept His commandments which the Lord had commanded Moses."[70] His piety reveals that God's people of any generation can, by divine grace, stand firm against the idolatrous pressures of sinful men. Hezekiah is to be credited for his flight from two dangerous sins: 1. Exalting Moses and the Nehushtan, and 2. Fearing the pressure of those who engaged in such idolatry. Whereas men of lesser metal would have gladly compromised in order to please the people, Hezekiah sought to *revere and honor the Lord and His word.*

One of the great advancements of the Protestant Reformation was its strong repudiation of any idolatry where Popes, kings, religious clergy, as well as the saints of the past and present were magnified above Christ. Of course, the Reformation did not extinguish all such idolatry (no generation in this life will), but this should remind us that reformation in the church is a continual process. In his appeal to Emperor Charles V, John Calvin offered this excellent and scathing rebuke of the dangers of man-worship:

"Then, what shall I say of the blasphemies which rung in the public hymns, and which no pious man is able to hear without the utmost

---

[70] 2 Kings 18:5–6: 5 He trusted in the LORD, the God of Israel; so that after him there was none like him among all the kings of Judah, nor among those who were before him. 6 For he clung to the LORD; he did not depart from following Him, but kept His commandments, which the LORD had commanded Moses.

horror? We all know the epithets which they applied to Mary — styling her the gate of heaven, hope, life, and salvation; and to such a degree of infatuation and madness had they proceeded, that they even gave her a right to order Christ! For still in many churches is heard the execrable and impious stanza, 'Ask the Father; command the Son.' In terms in no respect more modest do they celebrate certain of the saints, and these, too, saints of their own making, i.e., individuals whom they, on their own judgment, have admitted into the catalogue of saints. For, among the multitude of praises which they sing to Claud, they call him 'the light of the blind,' 'the guide of the erring,' 'the life and resurrection of the dead.' The forms of prayer in daily use are stuffed with similar blasphemies. The Lord denounces the severest threatenings against those who, either in oaths or in prayers, confounded his name with Balaam. What vengeance, then, impends over our heads when we not only confound him with saints as minor gods, but with signal insult rob Christ of the proper and peculiar titles with which he is distinguished, in order that we may bestow them on creatures? Were we to be silent here, also, and by perfidious silence call down on ourselves his heavy judgments?"[71]

Calvin's censures are strong, but needful. The excesses of his day were the culmination of Rome's longstanding descent into the cauldron of man-centered idolatry. As we mentioned before, these excesses did not take place overnight, but developed from the smallest mutations of worship from earlier generations. All of this reminds us that not even the best of God's messengers should become our object of hope, reverence, or worship; God alone deserves such devotion and no one else. Such lessons from the past continue on as pillars of warning for all succeeding generations, and it is imperative that we observe them carefully so as to walk circumspectly. The plain tutorial of human history is this: whether by fear or fawning devotion, our natural tendency is to exalt men

---

[71] John Calvin, *The Necessity of Reforming the Church* (Heraklion Press), Locations 1018-1019, Kindle Edition.

above the One who alone deserves such exaltation. From the fall of mankind to the present day, all of human history is a repeat of these same idolatrous tendencies. Thus, we see in all this a universal frailty and idolatrous tendency *to exalt men, relics, religious philosophies, and countless other inventions crafted by the art and thought of man.*[72] Should we ignore these important warnings, we will surely walk in a dangerous state of blindness, where we are unable to see our own sinful frailty. We should also note that, not only are we inclined to exalt mere men, but we also have the insidious inclination to exalt ourselves. After Christ observed His final Passover meal with the disciples, indicating that one would betray him, a dispute arose among them:

Luke 22:23–27: 23 And they began to discuss among themselves which one of them it might be who was going to do this thing. 24 And there arose also a dispute among them as to which one of them was regarded to be greatest. 25 And He said to them, "The kings of the Gentiles lord it over them; and those who have authority over them are called 'Benefactors.' 26 "But not so with you, but let him who is the greatest among you become as the youngest, and the leader as the servant. 27 "For who is greater, the one who reclines at the table, or the one who serves? Is it not the one who reclines at the table? But I am among you as the one who serves."

In all of this, we find a very strong inclination within the human heart to exalt the creature rather than the Creator, yet we are often unaware of these inclinations. It is for this reason that we must acknowledge that one of the greatest threats to the believer is this matter of *blindness to personal sin*. Like the patient who refuses care because he is in denial of his serious injuries, so is the believer who is in denial of his own serious, sinful tendencies. We become the greatest danger to ourselves when we live in such denial of sin,

---

[72] Acts 17:29.

however, no man in human history was ever exempt from such struggles. For the church in the present day, the challenges of celebritism and the fear of man continue, and they are prone to spread with great rapidity in this new age of new media. Should we ignore such problems, diminish their dangerous influences, or pretend that they hardly exist at all, we will prove ourselves to be presumptuous fools.

Several years ago, while ministering in Minnesota, I learned that one of my fellow classmates from seminary was moving to a nearby city in order to serve as a pastor. We'll call him Mark. Having had some time to get to know Mark in seminary, I can say that I was glad to have him as a new neighbor. We connected quickly when he arrived, and I recall taking a Sunday off in order to hear him preach just as he was beginning his ministry. He and his wife were an endearing, young couple that our family enjoyed. They had no children yet, but they were eager to start a family and they were excited to begin their new adventure serving Christ in their church. It may have been only a few months after Mark arrived that we both ran into an interesting ministry issue, though we didn't discover the simultaneity of our experiences right away. For the both of us, a very popular book had been introduced within our respective flocks to be used as teaching material. For myself, I knew little of the book or its author and was little prepared to offer an opinion as to whether or not the title would be useful. The few things that I did know about this book are as follows: *1. It was being published and promoted by Lifeway, a large and well known Christian publishing company whose support for this book was enormous in view of their extensive promotion of it; 2. Many in the church were greatly drawn to the author and were already familiar with some of his other published materials; and 3. The book was starting to go viral in many churches before the internet-colloquialism "viral" existed.* Admittedly, I allowed this broad ether of praise and accolades to influence my thinking. I thereby approved the request and an order was placed with the publisher for several copies. Everything was on track until someone raised some pointed questions about certain elements in the book. This led me to a deeper study and analysis of the material, culminating in the realization that I had failed to notice deeply problematic sections in the book that should not be ignored. While no book is perfect, save the Bible, I had to wrestle with the question of whether or not the book should be scrapped, or cautiously and selectively used. I spoke with the leadership about my concerns and the conclusion became rather clear: issue a correction on my original approval, cancel the order, and take the time to explain to those most affected why such a decision was best for the good of the church and the glory of Christ. Orders were cancelled, explanations were given and the flock received the adjustment quite well, with very few exceptions. Overall, this whole event became a good teaching opportunity for everyone, especially myself. However, Mark's church didn't have the same response.

At about the time that we as a church were moving beyond this celebrity-book debacle of my own making, I came to discover that Mark was having a similar encounter with the same material. Our experiences were nearly identical, except that Mark had developed a concern for the literature in question much more quickly than I did, and his congregation didn't respond well to his expressed concerns. When Mark contacted me about all this, I was able to share with him my own experiences. We discussed whether or not such material should be approved in good conscience, or if it would be worth a potential conflict within the church. Mark was very concerned, not only about the material (just as I was), but he was especially concerned about how some in the congregation were responding to the situation. Exceeding my own efforts, Mark not only taught through his concerns for several weeks, but he also developed a small booklet in which he addressed his concerns through a more direct teaching of the Scriptures. Upon reviewing his manuscript (which he requested for the sake of feedback and accountability), I wasn't at all surprised to find a deeply irenic tone in what he had written. Mark was very careful and gracious in his words and actions. Much prayer was offered up about the matter and we were hopeful that the Lord would use this conflict for the overall good and maturation of the flock. The details of what followed are too numerous for the purpose of this book, but it is enough to say that Mark's experiences with the church transformed into a nightmarish downgrade. Through the instigation and complaints of just a few prominent individuals within the church, Mark's efforts at leading and teaching the flock became a rather gruesome battle. Certain members in his church were very upset that he would dare express the concerns that he did. These individuals were incredulous that a young pastor would dare question a book that was written by such a *prominent and celebrated author*, and they spread their disgust and dismay throughout the congregation. With great craft and subtlety, several church members made light of Mark's teaching on this controversy, they mocked him for his youth, and belittled his efforts to warn the flock about the erroneous elements within the controversial book. These were difficult and penetrating experiences for Mark and his wife and, sadly, just 7 months after arriving in Minnesota, Mark was ejected from his pastorate.

All this over a single book!

The whole experience was devastating and quite remarkable. Mark's congregation did not give him a hearing because he dared to touch that which had become a golden calf within the church. The famous author and his book entered the church with a triumphant procession, replete with the heraldic signs and symbols of authority now honored by many in the modern day: *academic acclaim, mainline denominational backing, cross-denominational popularity, multiple published books from reputable publishing companies, and a strong reputation as a conference speaker.* Though this popular author was not known personally by anyone in the church, his influence prevailed over a young pastor whose simple desire was to teach his flock the truths of the Scriptures. What is even more problematic is the fact that Mark's story is just a drop in the bucket. As I continue to have the opportunity to speak with churches and pastors, I find that Mark's story is, in fact, a dark, disturbing, and non-ending re-run played out in churches who want their celebrities more than God's word.[73] In too many churches today, the nobility of the Berean spirit has been replaced with *the golden calf of celebritism.*

---

[73] The fact that brethren throughout history have endured persecution, often at the hands of religious men, is not at all new. As already mentioned, Flavel and Bunyan were persecuted as non-conformist preachers, and this posed no small challenge for them in their respective ministries. Thus, when these men wrote about the dangers of man-centered fear, they did so with an abundance of experience, as J. Stephen Yille has observed: "Such temptation (ungodly fear) is not a matter of mere conjecture for Flavel...In 1662 in England, Parliament passed an Act of Uniformity, requiring ministers (who had not received Episcopal ordination) to be re-ordained. It also required ministers to declare their consent to the entire Book of Common Prayer and their rejection of the Solemn League and Covenant. The Church of England ejected those ministers (including Flavel) who refused to conform; they became known as dissenters or nonconformists. After his ejection from public ministry in the town of Dartmouth, Flavel continued to meet secretly with his former church members in order to preach the Scriptures and administer the sacraments. But, when the Oxford Act prohibited all nonconformist ministers from living within five miles of towns that sent representatives to Parliament, Flavel was forced to move to a different village. His people still ventured to hear him preach in private homes or wooded areas; and he slipped regularly into Dartmouth to visit them. In 1687, the authorities finally permitted Flavel to resume preaching in public. He enjoyed this liberty until his death four years later at age sixty-four." J. Stephen Yuille, Preface

I am glad to report, however, that the story of Mark and his ejection from the pastorate does not end on a sad note. In fact, a note of celebration is in order for this important reason: Instead of giving into the fear of man, Mark stood by biblical principles and resisted those who sought to pressure him. What could have been a far more grievous conclusion to this story is a scenario where Mark might have succumbed to the fear of self-preservation, compromised biblical standards for a false peace, capitulated to his accusers in order to retain his position and salary, and continued on with a ministry of rank hypocrisy. Simply put, by God's grace alone Mark did not succumb to the deeds of the flesh, but pressed on in the power and leading of the Spirit. In the end, the fear of man and the selfish pursuit of self-preservation are not the works of the Spirit; instead they constitute the works of the flesh which mirror the deeds of the ungodly, as Flavel rightly teaches:

> "Let not your fear produce in you mischievous effects as their fear doth; to make you forget God, magnify the creature, prefer your own wits and policies to the Almighty Power and never-failing Faithfulness of God...The fear of God will swallow up the fear of man, a reverential awe and dread of God will extinguish the slavish fear of the creature..."[74]

---

in Triumphing over Sinful Fear by John Flavel, ed. J. Stephen Yuille (Grand Rapids, MI: Reformation Heritage Books), viii-ix. Though Mark's ejection from the pastorate does not directly comport with that of Flavel's (i.e., state sponsored persecution), there are stark comparisons that should not be ignored. In this contemporary-church age, men who stand fast on the authority of God's word can be swiftly ejected from the ministry with little consideration. Pastors who refuse to enter the broad way of superficial religion have become modern day nonconformists in many respects. The spirit of compromise found within many churches today has created a hostile environment for anyone who wishes to remain devoted to Christ and His authority alone. In the end, the pattern and effects of spiritual compromise remain the same in all generations.

[74] Flavel, A Practical Treatise of Fear, 244.

When men enter into the dark path of ungodly fear, they yield great damage to themselves and to Christ's body. Mark certainly suffered through this trial, but I can assure you that, in God's providence, it refined him for further ministry. What all brethren must understand is that, from the pulpit to the pew, contests like these force us all to resolve in our hearts and minds who it is that we shall reverence in the end: God or men. The Lord provides His people with such trials for the testing of their faith, producing endurance (James 1:3) and deeper maturity (James 1:4). Tests such as these compel us to face ourselves, our frailties, and our desperate and daily need for grace. At the most primitive level, it is important to remember that, without the grace of salvation, we would be powerless to fear God rather than men, as Bunyan reminds us:

> "No man brings this grace [godly fear] into the world with him. Everyone by nature is destitute of it; for naturally none fear God, there is no fear of God, none of this grace of fear before their eyes, they do not so much as know what it is; for this fear flows, as was showed before, from a new heart, faith, repentance and the like; of which new heart, faith, and repentance, if thou be void, thou art also void of this godly fear. Men must have a mighty change of heart and life, or else they are strangers to this fear of God."[75]

In all of this we must remember that, when we reverence God above men, it is a sign of God's work of grace in our hearts. Left to our own strength, we degrade to dangerous compromises of the heart. Thus, it is important that we remember that the battle of the flesh against the Spirit is a daily one. The inclinations of the flesh must be mortified by the Spirit and the word lest we degrade into ungodly

---

[75] Bunyan, *A Treatise of the Fear of God.*

thoughts and affections. Again, Bunyan directs our thoughts in this matter:

"Wouldest thou grow in this grace of fear? then keep always close to thy conscience the authority of the Word; fear the commandment as the commandment of a God both mighty and glorious, and as the commandment of a father, both loving and pitiful...Every grace is nourished by the Word, and without it there is no thrift[76] in the soul (Prov 13:13, 4:20-22; Deut 6:12)."[77]

We are encouraged to know that the Lord continually shepherds His people through the holy prodding of His word. Yet, for us to receive the profit of His direction, we must revere His authority: "...to this one I will look, To him who is humble and contrite of spirit, and who trembles at My word" (Isaiah 66:2:). Our Good Shepherd's desire for His people is that they would be found in His protective arms *forever*,[78] enveloped in His truth, fearing not this world but instead fearing Him who has the power and authority of judgment over all of mankind.[79] Only in our Savior's awesome presence can we be at rest with great joy; preferring Him above all others; adoring Him as none other; and reverencing His authority alone. As His sheep, we need these reminders continually, especially in light of our tendency to wander into places of danger through our own ungodly fears. Thus, Flavel is right when he says:

"The sinfulness of our fears lies in the inordinancy of them...to exalt the power of any creature by our fears, and give it such an ascendant over us, as if it had an arbitrary and absolute dominion over us, or over our comforts, to do with them what it pleased; this is to put the

---

[76] A fact or condition of thriving or prospering.

[77] Ibid., 62.

[78] Psalm 28:9: Save Thy people, and bless Thine inheritance; be their shepherd also, and carry them forever.

[79] Matthew 10:28.

72

creature out of its own class and rank, into the place of God, and is therefore a very sinful and evil fear. *To trust in any creature, as if it had the power of a God to help us, or to fear any creature, as if it had the power of a God to hurt us, is exceeding sinful, and highly provoking to God."*[80] (italics mine)

Overall, our awareness of such human frailty is needful. The heart's inclination towards man-centered celebritism should give us a sense of pause and caution lest we find ourselves demoting Christ and His word in subtle, yet dangerous ways. Within this modern age we find that men and their teachings can be spread and heralded at an astonishing rate through a wide array of media resources: published books, online articles, videos, audio messages etc. Though many of these resources can be remarkably sound and helpful, there is an even greater abundance of resources which contain seeds of error, some small and some quite large. When these resources are popular, it is as though they have been christened with a presumed Evangelical seal of approval. However, popularity is no standard of measurement for truth. In a society which exalts the idols of professional athletes, movie stars, politicians, and various other celebrities, the church must remember that *social prominence offers no objective measure of truth*. Not only is this the case when assessing individuals, but it also applies to the reputation of whole churches:

> Revelation 3:1: 1 "To the angel of the church in Sardis write: He who has the seven Spirits of God and the seven stars, says this: 'I know your deeds, that *you have a name that you are alive*, but you are dead." [italics mine]

Though Sardis had "a name" (reputation) for being a vibrant and growing church, the reality of their condition was quite the

---

[80] Flavel, <u>A Practical Treatise of Fear</u>, 249-50

opposite. Imagine touring the community of Sardis and asking the people about the church and its ministry: we would hear glowing praise concerning their growth and progress. However, the only assessment that must matter is the assessment of the Lord Jesus Christ. In view of this, Christ's address to the church at Sardis brings us back to the truth we have been reviewing: *we should be most interested in the Lord's truth and judgment of things rather than the popular opinions of men.* Yet, because of indwelling sin, we tend to elevate the latter over the former:

> 2 Corinthians 10:12: For we are not bold to class or compare ourselves with some of those who commend themselves; but when they *measure* [*metrountes*] themselves by themselves and compare themselves with themselves, they are without understanding.

Corinth's man-centeredness was rooted in their inclination to measure themselves by their own human standards. Paul's use of the word, *metrountes > metreō* [*measure*], from which we get the word *metrics*, reminds us that human standards of evaluation are useless because they are warped and mutilated by sin. The fallen descendants of Adam require no training or pressure to slip into this error of substituting God's standards of measurement with their own. This was the problem with the 1st century Jewish leaders; it was the root sin of those who worshipped Moses' brazen serpent; it was the problem with the church at Sardis and those who praised it; it was the same problem which Calvin faced amidst the heralding of relics and men during the Reformation; and it is the universal problem of all men when the metrics of God's word are ignored in the face of public acclaim and praise.

It may be tempting to seek the comfort of knowing that modern Evangelicalism hasn't fully descended into the aforementioned examples of historic idolatry. However much comfort this may give to some, I would assert that a standard which seeks to avoid the extreme apostasy of yesteryear is not a good standard for anyone. To say, approvingly, that modern Evangelicalism hasn't descended into the rank error of heresy would be like a patient seeking counsel from his doctor, only to receive the "good news" that he's not dead...*yet.* Who among us seeks medical advice in order to discern whether or not we are a corpse? When we are ill, medical advice is helpful if it offers the exposure of, at least, three things: *1. The cause of our illness, 2. The present state of our illness, and 3. The cure for our illness.* If we deny the disease, or ignore the state of our condition and refuse the cure, we resultantly give ourselves over to disease's power until it is too late. Yes, I am glad that the whole of modern Evangelicalism hasn't descended into the abyss of rank heresy, but I must express concern regarding its present prognosis and apparent trajectory. Though we may not find incense, prayer, or public worship being offered to the many celebrated leaders of the Evangelical world, there are other troubling signs of similar, unhealthy devotion. In order for the local church to escape the clutches of man-centeredness and celebritism, pastors and their congregations must be diligent to pursue the nobility of the Bereans. Ultimately, pastors have the highest burden and responsibility to lead by way of example in order to encourage others to pursue such a standard. However, pastors who are slavishly beholden to other men, institutions of renown, or even their own popularity and acclaim, can be certain that they will foster more of the same among those who follow their example. Such a pastor as this will eventually prove himself to be a hireling in one form or another. It is his responsibility to uphold the banners of *Solus Christus* and *Sola Scriptura* within the church so that Christ would have preeminence over all. Such a pastoral image as this is richly presented in *Pilgrim's Progress*, where Christian was brought to a portrait depicting one who was *"a very grave person...having eyes lifted up to heaven, the best of books in his hand, the law of truth was written upon his lips, the world was behind his back; he stood as if pleading with men, and a crown of gold did hang over its head."*[81] Such is a portrait of one who fixes his eyes on Jesus *alone,* is serious about His kingdom, and therefore has no desire to trifle with this world.

Simply put, it is the portrait of anyone who *joyfully reverences* Christ and trembles at His word.

---

[81] John Bunyan, *The Pilgrim's Progress.*

MY BANNER IS CHRIST

~ CHAPTER IV ~

SOLUS CHRISTUS

VERSUS MAN-CENTERED

PARTISANSHIP

God's gift of the Scriptures is a treasure of matchless worth, and it is our great privilege to herald His word in our homes, within the church, and before this world of darkness. As David reminded us of God's provision for His people in Psalm 60:4: *"You have given a banner to those who fear You, that it may be displayed because of the truth [Selah]."* His truth we need for every aspect of our lives, for without it we would perish in our affliction.[82] Unfortunately, our sinful weakness draws us away from such a reverent view of God's authority. It is our natural propensity to degrade to a child-like foolishness regarding the Lord's matchless worth and the inestimable value of His word. Everyone who has spent time with little children will understand that they have profound difficulty understanding the sentimental or monetary value of things. This is simply an inherent part of their youth and inexperience, and it is for this reason that parents must offer a patient and faithful tutelage to their young ones. If you hand a child an expensive and fragile item, don't be surprised when they look at it as nothing more than an interesting play-thing. Should they break it, they won't experience the grief that you will because of youthful naïveté. In the spiritual realm, we have a similar form of immaturity and naïveté concerning God's gifts. It is too easy to treat the gems and jewels that God has given to the church as common marbles and stones. It is for this reason that we constantly need to meditate on the value and worth of the riches which the Lord has lavished upon His church. Without such a regular meditation, we tend to degrade into a dangerous ignorance and indifference. Understanding this reality, the Apostle Paul wrote to the church at Ephesus, imploring them to flee such childishness in their pursuit of spiritual maturity:

---

[82] Psalm 119:92.

Ephesians 4:11–14: 11 And He gave some as apostles, and some as prophets, and some as evangelists, and some as pastors and teachers, 12 for the equipping of the saints for the work of service, to the building up of the body of Christ; 13 until we all attain to the unity of the faith, and of the knowledge of the Son of God, to a mature man, to the measure of the stature which belongs to the fullness of Christ. 14 As a result, we are no longer to be children, tossed here and there by waves, and carried about by every wind of doctrine, by the trickery of men, by craftiness in deceitful scheming;

In Ephesians 4, Paul sought to increase the Ephesian believers' comprehension of the Lord's gifts to the church. In his appeal for their increased maturity, he explained to them what it cost for the church to receive such divine gifts of grace: the sacrifice of the Son of God (Ephesians 4:7-10). Through His sacrificial gifts of apostles, prophets, evangelists, pastors and teachers, the church is supplied with what it needs in order to be equipped and built up in maturity. Thus, pastors and teachers must hold fast to that which the Lord has revealed and given to the church for all ages: God's holy word. When we fail to embrace God's provisions of grace and divine truth, then the trajectory of our lives leads to grave danger. The picture of being out to sea, tossed about by violent waves and wind, is a fitting one for those who depart from the security of God's word. Paul's lesson is quite simple: we will either pursue the surety of God's truth in the fear of Christ or be engulfed in the storms of worldly thinking and philosophies. The former pathway leads to "the unity of the faith" (v. 13), whereas the latter leads to utter ruin. Ultimately, the church is called to use God's gifts and provisions in order to preserve the unity of the church. This is not a mere option, it is the very mandate of God:

Ephesians 4:2–5: 2 with all humility and gentleness, with patience, showing forbearance to one another in love, 3 *being diligent to preserve the unity of the Spirit in the bond of peace.* 4 There is one body and one

Spirit, just as also you were called in one hope of your calling; 5 one Lord, one faith, one baptism... [italics mine]

It should be quite clear that the Lord prizes the unity of His church; after all, Christ laid down His life and *gave gifts* to the church for the preservation of such unity. He is the creator of such unity, *but we are called to preserve this unity with diligence, humility, patience, and forbearance – in love.* The cumulative message of these verses is quite powerful. It shows us that when we fail to pursue, with diligence, the unity of the faith in Christ's body, then we are behaving like foolish children who cast aside God's truth and grace in exchange for worldly things which lead to anarchy and ruin. The more I consider the compelling nature of Paul's instruction and warning, the more I am reminded of this compelling reality: *unity requires much effort along with the full spectrum of God's gifts to the church; however, division and destruction requires little effort at all.*

While serving as a young pastor in the Midwest many years ago, I found myself in the middle of a firestorm of theological contention. A number of people began to complain about what I had been teaching from the pulpit. Those who were agitated the most by my ministry were individuals who pushed back on any emphasis on God's sovereign work in salvation and the believer's calling to obey God's commands. The church had originated with teachings that had a disproportionate emphasis on dispensationalism and premillennialism with the kind of overemphasis on such doctrines which diminished core Gospel truths. The resultant theology which emanated from these early influences was that of a dangerous hyper-grace theology which undermines the truths of Christ's Lordship and His work of sanctification in the life of believers. This took place during the mid-90's when the "Lordship debate" was raging and, to provoke matters more, one of the church's previous pastors helped to fan the flames of discontentment by recommending antagonistic books to disgruntled church members. In one church meeting, I had the remarkable experience of being called an extremist and cultist without any actionable evidence to support the charge. While this contest continued to brew, I had received news that my father had passed away. I had no choice but to travel back to California in view of my mother's and sister's need for my immediate support and encouragement. Upon arriving, I discovered that my father, whose health had already been failing, made no provision for a will. Thus, the pain and stress of his death was compounded by the complexity of discerning what to do with his dwindled estate and remaining debts. On top of all this, I was numb with incredulity over the fact that my first funeral service as a pastor would be performed for my father who consistently rejected the Gospel throughout his life. When I returned home, not only was I emotionally and physically exhausted, but I was coldly greeted with a petition signed by some in the church demanding my resignation. Needless to say, this wasn't exactly the greeting that I had hoped to receive. I certainly knew that the struggles of our church wouldn't vanish while I was gone, but I was somewhat startled to find such a scandal waiting upon my return. Thus, upon my return from my father's funeral, I discovered that a fully trained and well equipped army of hyper-grace soldiers were waiting for me, ready to wage their well-planned war.

Yet the contest that these individuals sought was quite odd. Rather than addressing me and my teachings directly, most individuals criticized me in view of what they merely assumed I believed based upon the seminary I attended. Because of this there was little dialogue, but an abundance of presumption, judgment, and scolding from those who opposed me. Knowing the seminary I had attended, many of these individuals demanded that I answer for a number of things said and written by its president. It was striking to me that they eagerly quoted his sermons and books, in order to refute them, and they did so in a manner which seemed to presume that I too should have been equally familiar with his material. Additionally, our conversations often drifted from questions about the scriptures to debates about church history, especially the Reformation. With their heraldic, ideological banners raised, these battle-ready warriors had marked out their turf, not for a direct debate over what the Bible taught, but for a *proxy war* between their heroes of the faith versus those whom they presumed were my heroes. Despite my best efforts to the contrary, little civil discussion took place regarding what the Bible actually says. All of this was disheartening since, as previously mentioned, the church is powerless to pursue the unity of the faith without Holy Writ as her sole foundation and guide.

As an early experience in pastoral ministry, all this was highly instructive even though it was remarkably disturbing. It showed me that one of Satan's central tactics is to draw people from having honest and open discussions over God's word. He knows just how lethal Scripture is to his cause and for this reason he opposes *Sola Scriptura* out of his hatred of the church's priority of *Solus Christus.* In place of these priorities, our chief enemy is always eager to lift up a host of banners bearing the symbols of false authority: *ecclesiastical creeds, church history, oral traditions, manmade institutions, and academic acclaim.* Whenever and wherever he can substitute the true authority of Scripture with a counterfeit, then he has fulfilled his maniacal mission.

All of us should be reminded that it is our highest duty and privilege to seek the Lord and His word whenever we attempt to settle disputes, for anything less than this is a fool's errand. Yet, this is easier said than done. In the face of theological contests there will always be pressures, both external and internal, to conform one's thoughts to the opinions of men, but this must be vigorously resisted. We have already looked at some such pressures dealing with the sin of fearing men, but there are other issues that we ought to consider:

1. Man-Centered Partisanship: God's word divides truth from error and therefore it drives a clear wedge between the children of God and the children of the Devil.[83] It is in this sense that we must admit that divisions over the clear teachings of Scripture are necessary in a world of sin, apostasy, and unbelief.[84] Yet, *man-centered partisanship* represents a distraction from the Scriptures altogether, because it heralds the views of mere men above all. Like many other transgressions, this problem is as old as the fall itself and it reminds us that when men identify themselves with certain theological camps, it is not uncommon for pride and party-loyalty to reign in their thinking. The history of the Pharisees reveals much of this party-loyalty, especially in their rabbinic traditions as recorded in the Mishnah. It is here that we find, line after line, didactic statements prefaced with the textual heraldry of rabbinic authority: *"...the House of Shammai say...the house of Hillel say."* So important was this rabbinic partisanship to the Jewish people[85] that they had lost sight of the true authority of God, or as Christ said: *"neglecting the commandment of God, you hold to the tradition of men."*[86] Such theological partisanship was promoted among the Jewish people from their earliest days:

---

[83] 1 John 3:4-10.

[84] 1 Corinthians 11:19.

[85] "The Talmud records that 'two and a half years the School of Shammai and the School of Hillel were divided on the following point: The latter maintained that it had been better if man had never been created. The count was taken and the majority decided that it would have been better if he had not been created; but since he has been created, let him investigate his (past) actions. Another version is: Let him examine his (present) actions." Abraham Cohen, Everyman's Talmud – The Major Teachings of the Rabbinic Sages, (New York: Schocken Books, 1995), 95.

[86] Mark 7:6-9.

"Biblical passages which were interpreted in a Messianic sense afforded a variety of names by which he would be called. Certain Rabbinic students even exercised their ingenuity to discover for him a name similar to that borne by their teacher. 'What is the Messiah's name? The School of Rabbi Sheila said, "Shiloh, as it is written, 'Until Shiloh come' (Gen xlix. 10)." The School of Rabbi Jannai declared, "Jinnon, as it is said, 'His name shall be continued (Heb. *jinnon*) as long as the sun' (Ps. lxxii. 17)." The School of Rabbi Channina declared, "Chaninah, as it is said, 'I will show you no favour' (Heb. *chaninah*) (Jer. xvi. 13)." Others contend that his name is Menachem son of Hezekiah, as it is said, "The comforter (Heb. *menachem*) that should refresh my soul is far from me (Lament. i. 16)."[87] When we examine the Pharisees in this manner, we must avoid the error of thinking that they were cut out of some unique cloth of human sinfulness. As we have already observed, the errors of the past stand as pillars of warning for every sinful generation. Man-centered partisanship is a struggle common to all such that it can occur in churches that are even blessed with a uniquely undivided leadership and message:[88] *1 Corinthians 1:10–13: 10 Now I exhort you, brethren, by the name of our Lord Jesus Christ, that you all agree, and there be no divisions among you, but you be made complete in the same mind and in the same judgment.11 For I have been informed concerning you, my brethren, by Chloe's people, that there are quarrels among you.12 Now I mean this, that each one of you is saying, 'I am of Paul,' and 'I of Apollos,' and 'I of Cephas,' and 'I of Christ.'13 Has Christ been divided? Paul was not crucified for you, was he? Or were you baptized in the name of Paul?"* Corinth's conflict reminds us that we all have the fallen propensity to take sides and elevate certain personalities *for no good reason at all.* However, when there are disputes of substance, we must be careful not to be beholden to a man-centered theological partisanship which takes us away from an objective analysis of Scripture. From the past to the present, the lesson remains the same: A theology that is formed out of a plain and clear

---

[87] Cohen, <u>Everyman's Talmud</u>, 347.

[88] By speaking of a *"uniquely undivided leadership and message,"* I am referring to the unique position of Christ's Apostles.

exegesis of the Scriptures is what our souls desperately need, because it magnifies Christ and His authority; but a theology that is rooted in the priority of man-centered partisanship is the death knell to orthodoxy.

2. The Herd Mentality: One of the remarkable experiences that I have had in pastoral ministry over the years is the discovery of individuals who make spiritual choices on the sole foundation of what they see others doing, i.e., *the herd mentality.* The motives can vary, but the problem remains the same. The rule of life and conduct for the Christian is not to keep up with what others are doing, or as the expression goes: *keeping up with the Joneses.* Thus, the benchmark for truth is not horizontally defined, but is defined by Christ and His Word – *no matter what the Joneses are doing.* In our market-driven culture we frequently find whole neighborhoods following such a pattern of conformity. One neighbor buys a 60" flat panel TV; the other neighbors see it, want it, come to conclude that they *need it* and buy one themselves whether they will end up using it or not. Unfortunately, such choices can be dictated by pride, jealousy, or materialism (or all three) rather than by wisdom. When Christians make spiritual choices in a similar manner, it can be quite dangerous. Doing what one's friends or neighbors are doing is never a justification for *doing anything at all.* In this present culture of retail Christianity, I fear that many are determining orthodoxy by what is deemed as vogue among the masses; but this can never be the means by which we evaluate anything. In the worst of all cases, people can come to feel that without that next popular book, conference, or webinar – their sanctification will somehow be incomplete. Aware of these common thoughts and anxieties among the masses, the Christian industrial complex often preys on such fears. Though the retail earnings may be good for those who produce, promote, and distribute religious wares, such a spirit of *dependency* on such things is dangerous since it diminishes the primacy of Scripture and the local church. As already stated, it is not that all such resources are bad. There are many profitable resources out there that can be utilized for the glory of God. However, there are many well-marketed, well-polished, and highly praised resources that are deeply problematic. What is needed is for the believer to be dedicated to Christ with the nobility of those Bereans who "received the word with great eagerness, examining the Scriptures daily" in order to see if the teaching they received was true.[89] It is this attitude which says - "I must measure everything by the standard of God's Word, not by the standard of my neighbors, social popularity, or any mere man" - that Luke calls: "noble minded." However, had those Bereans of yesteryear simply kept up with the popular thinking of their day, they would have entered the broad way of the traditions and philosophies of mere men.

3. The Abuse & Misuse of Labels: Theological terms and labels are often extremely helpful if they are used with clarity and wisdom. A simple example of this point can be found in the term *Trinity*, which is very helpful in the matter of identifying the unified Godhead who subsists as Father, Son, and Holy Spirit. Without such a label for this precious scriptural truth, our task of describing the fullness of God's nature and person would be much more difficult. On the other hand, theological terms and labels can be abused, particularly when they are applied erroneously or imprecisely. This is especially true when it comes to the use of labels dealing with doctrinal movements from church history. For example, I have found that many people who deny the doctrines of grace will use the label *Hyper-Calvinism* as a strict synonym for *Calvinism* as if the two denoted the same thing, but this reveals a plain misunderstanding of church history. Over the years I have developed an increased concern over how the labels of church history often provide an unhelpful stumbling block amidst important discussions over biblical theology, especially when people don't have a sound understanding of church history to begin with. Many people who hear the name John Calvin, or the term *Calvinism*, immediately conjure the worst possible associations with such an identity based upon hearsay rather than actual history. As I have continued to preach

---

[89] Acts 17:10–11 (NASB) — 10 And the brethren immediately sent Paul and Silas away by night to Berea; and when they arrived, they went into the synagogue of the Jews.11 Now these were more noble-minded than those in Thessalonica, for they received the word with great eagerness, examining the Scriptures daily, to see whether these things were so.

the doctrines of God's sovereign grace over the years, I have been called a Hyper-Calvinist, a Calvinist-heretic, and even a Calvinist-cultist – even though it has not been my practice to use the label Calvinist. What has been so striking in all this is the discovery that too few people understand the history of the Reformation, Jacobus Arminius, and the Five Articles of Remonstrance. More important than church history itself, I have found that many of these same individuals do not understand the scriptural responses to the Five Articles of Remonstrance regarding *man's total depravity, God's unconditional election, Christ's particular redemption, God's irresistible grace, and the reality of the saint's perseverance by His sovereign grace.* On the other side of this problem, there are some whose focus on the Reformation and John Calvin is so slavish and intense that they seem to be more eager to be called a Calvinist than they are to be called a Christian. It is not uncommon to find that individuals like these are more inclined to quote a Reformer or a confession from the era than they are to quote Scripture itself. This too is idolatry. Such "Calvinists" as these should reconsider the true John Calvin from history. Calvin's zeal for evangelism, humility, and high regard for the authority of Scripture is all deeply encouraging. He had a vehement opposition against papalism and the adoration of mere men. He utilized the church fathers as mere guides to exegesis, but not as the final authorities of it. During Calvin's lifetime, the Roman Catholic Church had shown all of the signs of man-centeredness that one could possibly imagine, and Scripture had become an incidental decoration to Rome's masterpiece of man-made tradition. Priests recited, not the authority of God as their ultimate source of truth, but only those church fathers whose views favored their own. When one studies such severe adoration of mere men during this period, it is difficult to avoid comparisons to the Mishnaic writings of the Jews which heralded the various rabbinic schools and leaders of yesteryear. Amidst all this man-centeredness, Calvin refuted such slavery to tradition and hero worship by directing others to the Reformational concepts of *Sola Scriptura, Solus Christus, Sola Gratia, Sola Fide,* and *Soli Deo Gloria.* I would urge the reader to pick up a biography of John Calvin and discover how it is that he sacrificed much in his life in order to deter others from the man-worship that was so prevalent in his day. When one learns more about this soldier of Christ, it seems impossible to imagine that he would endure others going about identifying themselves by his name as their *chief identity*. Every man must choose the manner in which he describes and utilizes various theological labels, but I would urge caution over the danger of doing anything that would foster a real or perceived man-centered partisanship which stifles a central focus on Christ and the Scriptures. Those who treat the Reformation as an infallible event only add fodder to the canons of the critics of the Reformation. Church history is remarkably important, but its importance does not transcend Holy Writ itself. In all of this, we all must guard against the potential of placing unnecessary barriers before those who have yet to learn the biblical truths regarding of God's sovereign, redeeming, and sanctifying grace.

My aforementioned pastoral conflict was clearly exacerbated by all these components: *man-centered partisanship, the herd mentality, and the misuse of labels.* Each of these elements served as a restraint which held back the needed Berean activity of searching the Scriptures. Sadly, I witnessed people making dogmatic conclusions based upon theological-party loyalty, what their friends were doing, and what they had heard *by way of rumor* about the doctrines of grace and the Reformation. All of this undermined the principles of *Sola Scriptura* and *Solus Christus* and fomented a destructive division within the body. Of course, some division is needful and we have already noted that Scripture creates a regular divide between truth and error.[90] Moreover, Scripture is the very sword of the Spirit which will divide and separate some of the closest bonds known to mankind:

Matthew 10:34–40: 34 "Do not think that I came to bring peace on the earth; I did not come to bring peace, but a sword. 35 "For I came to SET A MAN AGAINST HIS FATHER, AND A DAUGHTER

---

[90] 1 Corinthians 11:19.

AGAINST HER MOTHER, AND A DAUGHTER-IN-LAW AGAINST HER MOTHER-IN-LAW; 36 and A MAN'S ENEMIES WILL BE THE MEMBERS OF HIS HOUSEHOLD. 37 "He who loves father or mother more than Me is not worthy of Me; and he who loves son or daughter more than Me is not worthy of Me. 38 "And he who does not take his cross and follow after Me is not worthy of Me. 39 "He who has found his life shall lose it, and he who has lost his life for My sake shall find it. 40 "He who receives you receives Me, and he who receives Me receives Him who sent Me."

Division is necessary when others seek to have us compromise or abandon the core truths of Scripture. It can even be necessary when individuals wish to divide over man-centered partisanship. Whatever our relationships with others may be, the believer's highest calling is to take up his cross and follow Christ in obedience to *His word.* Any form of theological partisanship which diminishes or impedes the principles of *Solus Christus* and *Sola Scriptura* must be resisted, even at the most personal level of our human bonds. Whatever allegiances we may have with men in this world, past or present, we must subjugate them all to our higher union with Christ. We must not only do this for the good of our own souls, but also for the good of others whom we influence. After all, the spiritual trajectory of one generation can very easily influence subsequent ones, and we should therefore dread the possibility of placing stumbling blocks before Christ's sheep, both now and in the future.

MY
BANNER
IS
CHRIST

~ CHAPTER V ~

YOU CANNOT

SERVE TWO

MASTERS

If we with humility, contrition, and reverence of heart tremble at God's word (Isaiah 66:2), then we flee from the temptation to wander from God's prescribed pathway of truth. However, when left to ourselves, our pride, arrogance, and irreverence, we are prone to stray from the King's highway just like Bunyan's characters: Simple, Sloth, and Presumption in *The Pilgrim's Progress*. These three men were found *just outside the King's highway, fast asleep, with fetters on their heels, and completely unaware of the danger they were in.* Bunyan's inclusion of these self-deceived travelers reminds us of the believer's need to reverence God's authority and remain vigilant in all aspects of life. By this he also reminds us that men are prone to stray from truth for various reasons, yet a common thread among all such departures is a dangerous lack of reverence for God and His word. Because of this, we must regularly revive our hearts to *rejoice with trembling* in our worship of the Lord, while resisting society's pressure to bow the knee to whatever is trending at any given moment.

If popularity were actually the arbiter of truth, then it would be our duty to identify and follow the masses wherever they may lead. However, this would be no simple task seeing that theological trends are slippery things. In a world of pluralistic philosophies and preferences, theological trends tend to come in multiple shapes and sizes. As well, what is in vogue today will most likely fade for a while until it becomes "new" again in another age. The prospect of chasing "truth" in an environment like this would be like chasing swine in a hog pen, with this single query: exactly which pig should one grab onto and take for a ride through the mud of human "wisdom?" Trend seekers never seem to be satisfied with the ancient, unchanging truth of God's word. For them, the immutable realities of Scripture seem to be of inferior rank to that of the passing whims and opinions of esteemed mortals. There is something within our natural, fallen composition which inclines us to be drawn to the shine and sheen of popular thinking, especially if it portends some form of hope for mankind. This is true today just as it has been throughout history. As noted earlier, the people of the 16th century celebrated the *false hope* of indulgences, the *heresy* of papal pardon, and the *Gospel destroying doctrine* of purgatory. Though these were the universal beliefs of the day, none of them were made true by the force of their popularity or religious backing. One thing that is for certain, these doctrines survived and thrived because they brought great influence, power, control, and financial gain to the Catholic Church.

Our earlier mention of Tetzel's sale of indulgences reveals much about the business of bad theology. If we were to delve further into the background of this story, we would also discover another significant individual worthy of mention: *Albert of Hohenzollern.* Albert was an ambitious religionist who, by way of simony, purchased the bishopric of Magdeburg along with the archbishopric of Mainz. In view of the massive debt accrued for these purchased offices, Albert devised a plan to raise the funds needed to pay off his loans through the sale of indulgences. Having permission from Pope Leo X to do so, Albert was called upon to carry out his plan with the understanding that half of the monies he acquired would go to the Papacy while he retained the other half. Thus, needing a shrewd and effective salesman, Albert commissioned Johan Tetzel to promote the sale of these papal-approved indulgences. Albert equipped Tetzel with specific instructions that were designed to help increase indulgence sales called the "Summary Instruction,"[91] and this document promised

---

[91] Hans J. Hillerbrand, The Reformation – A narrative history related by contemporary observers and participants, (New York: Harper & Row Publishers, 1964), 39.

four "principal graces" to the purchaser: *1. The grace of forgiveness; 2. A letter of indulgence confirming rightful ownership of the indulgence; 3. The bestowal of the church's righteous merit to the purchaser of the indulgence along with their deceased relatives; and 4. Pardon for the souls of those now suffering in Purgatory.* A fairly detailed fee schedule was established for all members of society, from the members of royalty all the way down to mere peasants.[92] If one were to remove the doctrines of Purgatory and papal indulgences, then the coffers of Rome would run dry. In his book, *Roman Catholicism,* Loraine Boettner aptly describes the heart of Rome's financial engine:

> "The doctrine of purgatory has sometimes been referred to as 'the gold mine of the priesthood' since it is the source of such lucrative income. The Roman Church might well say, 'By this craft we have our wealth.'"[93]

In the end, *bad doctrine* has been *good business* since the fall of man, and we have an abundance of illustrations of this point in the modern day. In 2011, the Evangelical world was given one such illustration by means of a rather odd series of events. Controversial pastor and teacher Rob Bell had introduced his upcoming book, *Love Wins, via* a brief video in which he teased viewers with a series of cryptic questions about the afterlife. Though I wasn't all that familiar with Bell at the time, I knew that he came from the problematic pedigree of the Emergent Church movement. Knowing that I couldn't ignore the growing hype surrounding the book, I begrudgingly read the book when it was released. Bell's book posited a fairly familiar view of purgatory, one that was strikingly similar to that of C.S. Lewis. Thus, when I consulted the bibliography of *Love Wins,* I found just what I expected: a

---

[92] Ibid.

[93] Boettner, <u>Roman Catholicism</u>, 222.

reference to C.S. Lewis' fictional book, *The Great Divorce*. For those unfamiliar with church history and the Roman Catholic doctrine of purgatory, Bell's teaching most likely appeared to be quite dynamic and new. Others, failing to discern the vagaries of Bell's writing, had prematurely assumed that he was teaching universalism.[94] By itself, Bell's book was certainly problematic, yet reactions to what he wrote were even more problematic and even ironic. I say *ironic* because many of Bell's greatest critics also happen to be the loudest advocates of C.S. Lewis, whose theology of purgatory was no less dangerous than that of Bell's. In 1998, J.I. Packer noted the irony of C.S. Lewis' popularity within Evangelicalism, despite his views on purgatory *and many other things*:

"By ordinary evangelical standards, his [Lewis'] idea about the Atonement (archetypal penitence, rather than penal substitution), and his failure ever to mention justification by faith when speaking of the forgiveness of sins, and his apparent hospitality to baptismal regeneration, and his noninerrantist view of biblical inspiration, plus his quiet affirmation of purgatory[95] and of the possible final salvation of

---

[94] Those who prematurely accused Bell of being a Universalist failed to notice that what he wrote in *Love Wins* lacked the requisite clarity and consistency for such a judgment. If Bell's book is guilty of anything, it is guilty of being a confused and incoherent composition. His inductive methodology leaves the reader with more questions than answers, which is consistent with the methods of many Emergent Church. Rather than seeking the definitive answers of Scripture, Bell enjoys playing in the text of Scripture like a child in a sand box. For him, what is more important than the discovery of absolute truth is the priority of triggering new curiosities. It may be the case that Bell has now achieved the dogma and clarity of thinking needed to merit the label, Universalist, but this would only be a guess. The one thing that he did assert, with repeated dogma, is that those who pass from this life have a second chance, by being reconciled to God through purgatorial suffering.

[95] When speaking of his belief in Purgatory, he envisioned the purification process as follows: "I assume that the process of purification will normally involve

some who have left this world as nonbelievers, were weaknesses; they led the late, great Martyn Lloyd-Jones, for whom evangelical orthodoxy was mandatory, to doubt whether Lewis was a Christian at all. His closest friends were Anglo-Catholics or Roman Catholics;[96] his parish church, where he worshiped regularly, was 'high'; he went to confession; he was, in fact, anchored in the (small-c) 'catholic' stream of Anglican thought, which some (not all) regard as central. Yet evangelicals love his books and profit from them hugely."[97]

Packer's observations should make us wonder how much "profit" can be gained from a man whose writings were underscored with such doctrinal confusion. I addressed this entire subject in 2011 in my book, *Altar to an Unknown Love: Rob Bell, C.S. Lewis, and the Legacy of the Art and Thought of Man,* and therefore will here limit my comments, but it is important to note that Lewis' friendliness towards elements of Roman Catholic theology is far more significant than many Protestants realize. However, a number of Roman Catholic theologians have noticed this Catholicity in Lewis and rightly see him as a literary bridge back to Rome. Two notable books on this subject are *C.S. Lewis for the Third Millennium* by Peter Kreeft and *C.S. Lewis and the Catholic Church* by

---

suffering. Partly from tradition; partly because most real good that has been done me in this life has involved it. But I don't think suffering is the purpose of the purgation. I can well believe that people neither much worse nor much better than I will suffer less than I or more. 'No nonsense about merit.' The treatment given will be the one required, whether it hurts little or much. My favourite image on this matter comes from the dentist's chair. I hope that when the tooth of life is drawn and I am 'coming round,' a voice will say, 'Rinse your mouth out with this.' This will be Purgatory. The rinsing may take longer than I can now imagine." C.S. Lewis, *Letters to Malcolm: Chiefly on Prayer* (Houghton Mifflin Harcourt, 2002), Kindle Edition.

[96] Lewis reveals his syncretistic perspective concerning Roman Catholic dogma: "There are three things that spread the Christ-life to us: baptism, belief, and that mysterious action which different Christians call by different names-Holy Communion, the Mass, the Lord's Supper." C.S. Lewis, <u>Mere Christianity</u>, (New York: HarperOne), 61.

[97] Packer, <u>Surprised by Lewis</u>, 1998.

Joseph Pearce. Applauding such a covert and inceptive influence, Pearce issued the following quote from Lewis:

"Any amount of theology can now be smuggled into people's minds under cover of romance without their knowing it."[98]

This quote of Lewis explains, in part, why it is that many individuals who read Lewis' fictional works fail to notice, quickly, the defects of his theology. Most are typically shocked when they do discover Lewis' troubling convictions. Within an environment of such naiveté, Lewis' incipient influences aren't easily detected. His fictional works are designed to sway readers towards his theological thinking "without their knowing it," by his own admission. A great part of this agenda of his was to pass on the influences of his "Master," George MacDonald who was a Universalist and treated the doctrines of grace with remarkable disdain:

"...I have never concealed the fact that I regarded him [MacDonald] as my master; indeed I fancy I have never written a book in which I did not quote from him. But it has not seemed to me that those who have received my books kindly take even now sufficient notice of the affiliation. Honesty drives me to emphasize it."[99]

This little known admission by Lewis explains why it is that he, when advancing his views on purgatory in *The Great Divorce*, staged a fictional dialogue with George MacDonald over the subject of Universalism. Within that fictional dialogue, Lady

---

[98] "The Collected Letters of C.S. Lewis - Books, Broadcasts, and the War 1931-1949," Vol II Ed. Walter Hooper in <u>C.S. Lewis and the Catholic Church</u>, Joseph Pearce, (Ignatius Press, San Francisco, 2003), 78.

[99] C. S. Lewis, <u>George MacDonald, An Anthology</u> (New York: HarperCollins, 1946), xxxiii-xxxiv.

Julian[100] is quoted in order to suggest that purgatory may someday be wholly emptied and all will be saved in the end.[101] Like Bell, Lewis never lands on a definitive conclusion about the doctrine of Universalism in *The Great Divorce*. Lewis' efforts to promote his belief in purgatory, while raising questions about the possibility of Universalism, have been quite influential among many, and Rob Bell is just another illustration of such influence. Additionally, not only does Lewis promote the doctrine of purgatory in *The Great Divorce*, but he also issues explicit support for the doctrine in *Mere Christianity*,[102] and in *Letters to Malcom*.[103] Sadly, Lewis' admitted smuggling operation continues to thrive in the present day.

---

[100] Lady Julian, or Julian of Norwich, was a 14th century Catholic mystic and anchoress in England who believed that she received direct revelations from Christ. The section which Lewis has MacDonald quoting in the Great Divorce comes from Julian's work, *Revelations of Divine Love*: "But Jesus, who in this Vision informed me of all that is needful to me, answered by this word and said: "It behoved that there should be sin; but all shall be well, and all shall be well, and all manner of thing shall be well."

[101] Lewis: "In your own books, Sir," said I, "you were a Universalist. You talked as if all men would be saved. And St. Paul too."; MacDonald: "Ye can know nothing of the end of all things, or nothing expressible in those terms. It may be, as the Lord said to the Lady Julian, that all will be well, and all will be well, and all manner of things will be well. But it's ill talking of such questions."; Lewis: "Because they are too terrible, Sir?"; MacDonald: "No. Because all answers deceive. If ye put the question from within Time and are asking about possibilities, the answer is certain. The choice of ways is before you. Neither is closed. Any man may choose eternal death. Those who choose it will have it. But if ye are trying to leap on into Eternity, if ye are trying to see the final state of all things as it will be (for so ye must speak) when there are no more possibilities left but only the Real, then ye ask what cannot be answered to mortal ears." C.S. Lewis, <u>The Great Divorce</u> (Macmillan Publishing Co., Copyright 1946, New York, 1976 - Nineteenth Printing), 124-125.

[102] "Whatever suffering it may cost you in your earthly life, *whatever inconceivable purification it may cost you after death*, whatever it costs Me, I will never rest, nor let you rest, until you are literally perfect...As a great Christian writer (George MacDonald) pointed out, every father is pleased at the baby's first attempt to

On the one hand we could minimize such concerns and set them aside as an irrelevance, or we could acknowledge the lurking danger that men like Lewis pose within the church. If Lewis had little popularity in the modern day, we could offer less attention to his legacy. However, we find that Lewis has an ongoing influence within modern Evangelicalism that continues to accelerate in the present day:

"Since his death in 1963, sales of his books have risen to 2 million a year, and a recently polled cross section of ct [Christianity Today] readers rated him the most influential writer in their lives—which is odd, for they and I identify ourselves as evangelicals, and Lewis did no such thing. He did not attend an evangelical place of worship nor fraternize with evangelical organizations."[104]

Packer's observations of Lewis and his posthumous popularity should be alarming, especially in light of Lewis' admitted efforts to smuggle his views into the minds of his vast readership. In all of this we see the ongoing, transitive influences of George MacDonald and C.S. Lewis continuing on in men like Rob Bell *and many others in the modern day.* Bell's and Lewis' teaching on purgatory is dangerous for several reasons. *First,* the doctrine of purgatory posits the false hope that sinners can receive a second chance after this life. Those who believe in purgatory are inclined to think that, if their spiritual state is not cleared up before death, then it can be cleared up post-mortem through the sinner's

---

walk: no father would be satisfied with anything less than a firm, free, manly walk in a grown-up son." Lewis, Mere Christianity, 202-203, italics mine.

[103] "The right view [of Purgatory] returns magnificently in Newman's Dream. ...Religion has reclaimed Purgatory. *Our souls demand Purgatory, don't they?*" Lewis, *Letters to Malcolm*, italics mine.

[104] J.I. Packer, Still Surprised by Lewis: *Why This Nonevangelical Oxford Don Has Become Our Patron Saint,* (Christianity Today Online, September 7th, 1998).

atonement through intense suffering. How many souls will burn in Hell beneath such a damnable pretense as this, we cannot now know, however, the spiritual lethality of this doctrine should be self-evident. *Second*, like the doctrine of indulgences, purgatory is a form a teaching which undermines the Gospel and the principle of *Solus Christus* by gutting the *sole sufficiency* of Christ's work on the cross. By comparison, we can recall the Judaizers at Galatia who preached Christ *plus circumcision* as the grounds of the sinner's salvation. In such a Christ-*plus* scheme such as this, the Lord Jesus could no longer be the Redeemer *alone*. Similarly, purgatory claims that sinners can eventually be saved, but only at the *shared expense* of Christ *plus* the sinner's own suffering and purification, post-mortum. This too is a Christ-*plus* scheme. It is an alternate "Gospel," which is no true Gospel at all and warrants the anathema of God.[105] Loraine Boettner expands upon the insidious nature of the doctrine of Purgatory:

"Under the shadow of such a doctrine [purgatory] death is not, as in evangelical Protestantism, the coming of Christ for His loved one, but the ushering of the shrinking soul into a place of unspeakable torture. It is no wonder that millions of people born in the Roman Catholic Church, knowing practically nothing about the bible but believing implicitly in the doctrines of their church, should live and die in fear of death, in fear of spending an unknown number of years in the pain and anguish of that place called purgatory. How tragic that these people live in fear and servitude to the priests, who they are taught to believe hold in their hands the power of life and death, when all the time Christ has paid for their redemption *in full*."[106]

"It is safe to say that no other doctrine of the Church of Rome, unless it be that of auricular confession, has done so much to pervert the Gospel

---

[105] Galatians 1:8: But even if we, or an angel from heaven, should preach to you a gospel contrary to what we have preached to you, he is to be accursed!

[106] Boettner, Roman Catholicism, 219-20.

or to enslave the people to the priesthood as has the doctrine of purgatory.[107]

The dangerous doctrine of purgatory remains as a stronghold within Roman Catholicism in view of the ecclesiastical control it wields over the people. However, within Evangelicalism it would appear that purgatory is being promoted for different reasons: *book sales.* Doctrinally speaking, we must wonder why any professed Evangelical publishing company would sell such Purgatory-promoting wares. HarperCollins, the publisher of Rob Bell's book, *Love Wins,* has also published C.S. Lewis titles for years. It is in this sense that the sordid gain derived from a sordid doctrine continues within modern Evangelicalism. When men tremble well at the authority of God's word (Isaiah 66:2) they will not be tempted to add to His word. However, when men are filled with ungodly fear, they will not only add to God's word, but will gladly collect their thirty shekels of silver for their doctrinal creations. One thing that seems to be certain in the retail-driven world of modern publishing is that the *bottom line* is not truth, *but sales.* When visiting local Christian bookstores, it seems evident just how much of a hot ticket bad theology is within our shallow religious culture. Bestsellers are most often displayed prominently in such stores surrounded with colorful promotions from their publishers. The books themselves are often adorned with the heraldic signs and symbols germane to the publishing world: *big name endorsements, best-seller awards, and author-bios which sound nearly angelic.* Sadly, when one strips away such market-driven signs and symbols, very little substance is left with many of these modern titles. This is not to say that everything new is bad, but it is to say that not all that is celebrated by men is necessarily good and profitable to the souls of men. In view of this, I often

---

[107] Ibid, 222.

consider the thoughts of Samuel Davies (1723–1761) who said: "The venerable dead are waiting in my library to entertain me and relieve me from the nonsense of surviving mortals." Davies' words remind us that ours is not the only generation having to endure the doctrinal fluff that is too frequently celebrated among men. If there is money to be made, we can be sure that bad theology will always be available for mass consumption. The root of this is not a love for truth, but a love for mammon:

> 1 Timothy 6:3–10: 3 If anyone advocates a different doctrine and does not agree with sound words, those of our Lord Jesus Christ, and with the doctrine conforming to godliness, 4 he is conceited and understands nothing; but he has a morbid interest in controversial questions and disputes about words, out of which arise envy, strife, abusive language, evil suspicions, 5 and constant friction between men of depraved mind and deprived of the truth, who suppose that godliness is a means of gain. 6 But godliness actually is a means of great gain when accompanied by contentment. 7 For we have brought nothing into the world, so we cannot take anything out of it either. 8 If we have food and covering, with these we shall be content. 9 But those who want to get rich fall into temptation and a snare and many foolish and harmful desires which plunge men into ruin and destruction. 10 For the love of money is a root of all sorts of evil, and some by longing for it have wandered away from the faith and pierced themselves with many griefs.

According to Paul, godliness is a means of great gain, yet the gain of which he speaks is not the fleshly pursuit of wealth by means of corrupted teaching. The problem is not money itself but rather *the love of it* along with its attending *lack of love for truth.* There is a reason why the expression, *follow the money,* exists: it is because money trails often lead us to the sinful acts and passions of unprincipled men who wish to serve mammon rather than God. Yet, our Savior reminds us that we cannot serve God and mammon.[108] Worldly wealth always bears the dangerous potential of leading men astray from that which truly matters. Jude's warnings concerning Balaam remind us that men are easily drawn to the pathway which leads to the love of money and religious pandering: *"...for pay they have rushed headlong into the error of Balaam..." Jude 11.* Though this is the pathway of the world, it is not the pathway for the lovers of Christ. If we bear the name of Christ at all, it must be His banner that we herald above all rather than the multiple banners of this world, no matter how profitable they may be. For the Christian, the bottom line is not *mammon* but *Solus Christus and Sola Scriptura.* Without His riches, we are utterly bankrupt.

In conclusion, I offer to the reader Bunyan's timeless wisdom on this important subject. Remembering that he wrote and compiled *Pilgrim's Progress* while imprisoned for preaching the Gospel, we see that he had much time to contemplate the world's inverted value system. Upon this reflection, Bunyan wrote of a place that abounded in worldly wealth called Vanity Fair which was planted by the enemy on the main highway in order to tempt Pilgrims journeying towards heaven (the Celestial City):

> "It beareth the name of Vanity Fair, because the town where it is kept is lighter than vanity, Psa. 62:9; and also because all that is there sold, or that cometh thither, is vanity; as is the saying of the wise, "All that cometh is vanity." Eccl. 11:8... Almost five thousand years ago there were pilgrims walking to the Celestial City, as these two honest persons are: and Beelzebub, Apollyon, and Legion, with their companions, perceiving by the path that the pilgrims made, that their way to the city lay through this town of Vanity, they contrived here to set up a fair; a

---

[108] Matthew 6:24

fair wherein should be sold all sorts of vanity, and that it should last all the year long."[109]

As the main characters Christian and Faithful entered the city, they were accosted and pressed by the merchants of Vanity Fair. They were mocked and ridiculed for their failure to fit in, for their inability to speak the local language, and especially for their unwillingness to participate in any form of business. To these accusations, Christian had but one response:

"We buy the truth"[110]

If we truly believe in upholding the priorities of *Solus Christus* and *Sola Scriptura*, then we too must confess – *"we buy the truth"* and *nothing else.*

---

[109] See also 1:2–14; 2:11–17; Isa. 40:17. Bunyan, *The Pilgrim's Progress.*

[110] Proverbs 23:23: Buy truth, and do not sell it, Get wisdom and instruction and understanding.

MY BANNER IS CHRIST

~ CHAPTER VI ~

SOLUS CHRISTUS

IN THE LAND OF SODOM

AND GOMORRAH

Like *Vanity Fair*, the world in which we live continues to proffer its ungodly wares, yet we must be committed to *buying truth alone*. It is a great challenge to discern and tease out those influences that appear to be helpful, but instead incline us to stray from God's pathway with remarkable stealth. Whether by the printed page, video stream, or any other means, we are surrounded by countless counselors who seek to advise and direct. Whatever they have to say, we must always remember that Scripture *alone* must chart the course of our lives. As we press on in the Lord's prescribed pathway, we may find ourselves losing the *preferments and honours* of mere men, or we may even *face persecution*, but such matters must never deter the soldier of Christ. Flavel well understood such trials himself:

> "...there is no temptation in the world that hath overthrown so many, as that which hath been backed and edged with fear: the love of preferments and honours hath slain its thousands, but fear of sufferings its ten thousands."[111]

In the end, our subjection and servitude in the fear of Christ must never be supplanted by our regard for mere men. As the men of this world proceed from bad to worse,[112] we must remember that all who desire to live godly in Christ Jesus will be persecuted.[113] I find these reminders to be remarkably needful and helpful, especially since our nation has recently entered into a new phase of enmity with God and His word. On June 26th 2015, the Supreme Court of the United States announced its ruling that "same sex marriage" cannot be prohibited by any state in the Union. By this single act, a slim majority of unelected judges had thereby created an impotent mandate opposing God and the first of all His

---

[111] Flavel, <u>A Practical Treatise of Fear</u>, 277.

[112] 2 Timothy 3:13.

[113] 2 Timothy 3:12.

institutions – *the institution of marriage*. While believers rightly mourned this irreverent act of rebellion against the Creator, our nation's president, who repeatedly identifies himself as a Christian, proudly celebrated the court's decision by having the White House lit up like a LGBT flag. What this portends for the future no one can say for sure, but it does appear that things are proceeding from bad to worse[114] based upon the trajectory of recent history. Exactly two years prior to this judgment by America's highest court, another significant ruling was made against the institution of marriage. On June 26th 2013, the Supreme Court ruled against The Defense of Marriage Act (DOMA), a law which simply asserted that marriage was the union between one man and one woman.[115] Justice Antonin Scalia wrote a response against the majority ruling in which he rebuked the "high-handed" attitude of those who so eagerly undermined the institution of marriage:

> "To question its high-handed invalidation of a presumptively valid statute is to act (the majority is sure) with the purpose to 'dis-parage,' 'injure,' 'degrade,' 'demean,' and 'humiliate' our fellow human beings, our fellow citizens, who are homo-sexual. All that, simply for supporting an Act that did no more than codify an aspect of marriage that had been unquestioned in our society for most of its existence— indeed, had been unquestioned in virtually all societies for virtually all of human history. It is one thing for a society to elect change; it is another for a court of law to impose change by adjudging those who oppose it *hostis humani generis, enemies of the human race*."[116]

Scalia's observations are quite interesting, if not ironic, especially when we consider his use of the expression, *hostis humani generis*

---

[114] 2 Timothy 3:13.

[115] DOMA was originally passed on September 21st 1996.

[116] National Journal: Scalia: 'High-Handed' Kennedy Has Declared Us 'Enemies of the Human Race', http://www.nationaljournal.com/domesticpolicy/scalia-high-handed-kennedy-has-declared-us-enemies-of-the-human-race-20130626.

– *enemies of the human race.* Though he may not have intended the association, Scalia's use of this Latin expression brings to mind a similar expression used by Tacitus when describing Nero's persecution of the Christian community in the 1st century:

> "But neither human resources, nor imperial munificence, nor appeasement of the gods, eliminated sinister suspicions that the fire had been instigated. To suppress this rumour, Nero fabricated scapegoats – and punished with every refinement the notoriously depraved Christians (as they were popularly called). Their originator, Christ, had been executed in Tiberius' reign by the governor of Judaea, Pontius Pilatus. But in spite of this temporary setback the deadly superstition had broken out afresh, not only in Judaea (where the mischief had started) but even in Rome. All degraded and shameful practices collect and flourish in the capital. First, Nero had self-acknowledged Christians arrested. Then, on their information, large numbers of others were condemned - not so much for incendiarism as for their *hatred of humanity (odio humani generis).*[117] Their deaths were made farcical. Dressed in wild animals' skins, they were torn to pieces by dogs, or crucified, or made into torches to be ignited after dark as substitutes for daylight."[118]

Tacitus' description of these early Christians reveals how they were poorly viewed within the Greco-Roman world *as the haters of humanity.* The most likely explanation for this label is that the Christian community resisted, for conscience' sake, the hedonistic and idolatrous culture of the Greco-Roman world replete with its sacrifices to the gods and licentious living often associated with

---

[117] Scalia's reference to *hostes humani generis,* though strikingly similar in meaning, is probably rooted in maritime history, rather than being a quote from the ancient Roman historian.

[118] Tacitus, The Annals of Imperial Rome (New York: Barnes & Noble Books, 1993), 365, italics mine.

such worship.[119] Such opposition to idolatry was seen as an act of hostility against others, especially since the superstitious and pagan world believed that sacrifices to the gods were necessary for the greater good of the broader community.[120] Such opposition to pagan worship made the disciples the perceived enemies of the state. Though this reputation was remarkably unfair, it did point to the integrity of many believers who heralded a clear and strong Gospel witness in view of their unwillingness to compromise on the priority of *exalting Christ and His authority*. I would suggest that these historic points of interest offer a preview of what may come in the future. Apart from God's merciful and gracious intervention in America's apparent moral and spiritual suicide, further darkness will prevail in this land. Because of this, we must look to our Father with filial fear, lest we shrink back from the violent storms of this world, as Flavel said:

"It cannot be said of any man, as it is said of Leviathan, Job xli. 33 that he is made without fear; those that have most fortitude are not without some fears; and when the church is in the storms of persecution, and almost covered with the waves, the stoutest passengers in it may suffer as much from the boisterous passion within, as from the storm without; and all for want of thoroughly believing, or not seasonably remembering that, the Lord high Admiral of all the ocean, and

---

[119] Minucius Felis: "You apprehensive and anxiety-ridden Christians abstain from innocent pleasures. You don't watch the public spectacles, you don't take part in the processions, you absent yourselves from the public banquets, you shrink away from sacred games, sacrificial meat, and altar libations. That's how frightened you are of the gods whose existence you deny!" Minucius Felix, Octavius 8.4, 5; 9.2, 4-7; 10.2, 5; 12:5.

[120] "...The existence of the gods depends to an appreciable extent on man's devotion to them. Varro puts this quite simply when he writes: 'I am afraid that some gods may perish simply from neglect.'" Robert Maxwell Ogilvie, The Romans and Their Gods (New York: WW Norton & Company, 1969), 42.

Commander of all the winds, is on board the ship, to steer and preserve it in the storm."[121]

It is for this reason that believers must be resolved to stand firm in the strength of the Lord's might in order to fight the good fight of faith. Rather than shrinking back from the intense front lines of spiritual battle, in the fear of man, the church must press on with Christ's banner (*Solus Christus*) on the basis of His authority *alone* (*Sola Scriptura*). The wicked choices recently made by our nation, though sad, should be seen as an opportunity to magnify Christ's radiant glory amidst such a world of darkness. Moreover, the subject of marriage must not be avoided as if it were some ancillary point of doctrine with respect to the Gospel. Doing so would forsake many rich opportunities to magnify Christ, seeing that the Scriptures repeatedly associate the institution of marriage with the Lord's redemption of His people. Should anyone doubt this statement, they must consult the prophets Hosea (Hosea 2:19), Isaiah (Isaiah 62:4-5), and Jeremiah (31:31-34); King Solomon (Song of Solomon 8:6); and the Apostle Paul (Ephesians 5:22-33). Moreover, John the Baptist's confession of humility, as mentioned in the introduction, also happens to be rooted in the metaphor of *holy matrimony*:

> John 3:29–30: 29 "He who has the bride is the bridegroom; but the friend of the bridegroom, who stands and hears him, rejoices greatly because of the bridegroom's voice. And so this joy of mine has been made full. 30 "He must increase, but I must decrease."

Moreover, it is the true church's ultimate longing to be joined with her Bridegroom in His eternal kingdom (Revelation 19:7-10). In all of this it is quite clear that, from the Old Testament to the New Testament, the doctrine of marriage is no ancillary subject with

---

[121] Flavel, A Practical Treatise on Fear, p. 242.

respect to the Gospel. If we follow the teachings of the Scriptures, while heralding Christ and His authority alone, *then it is impossible to avoid this relationship between marriage and the Gospel.* It is in this sense that our nation's recent debates over homosexuality should be seen as an opportunity for the Gospel rather than as a reason to hide. In view of the church's current circumstances, she will most likely face further hostility in the future, but we must not be surprised by this.[122] We must seek to be at peace with all men,[123] but never at the expense of the truth,[124] remembering that we as servants are not above our persecuted and crucified Lord and Master:

> John 15:19–20: 19 "If you were of the world, the world would love its own; but because you are not of the world, but I chose you out of the world, therefore the world hates you. 20 "Remember the word that I said to you, 'A slave is not greater than his master.' If they persecuted Me, they will also persecute you; if they kept My word, they will keep yours also."

The church in America has reached a new crossroads such that she must stand for truth while resisting compromise before a watching world. The lines of separation continue to be made all the more clear in our society, but this offers us an even greater opportunity to make it clear that we are citizens of heaven and soldiers of the cross.

Yet we must consider another landmark event related to the homosexual debate. This one has nothing to do with the Supreme Court, but has everything to do with the question of the church's Gospel witness within a nation that is going the way of Sodom and

---

[122] 1 John 3:13: Do not marvel, brethren, if the world hates you.

[123] Romans 12:17-18.

[124] Matthew 10:34-37.

Gomorrah. The event in question took place just months before DOMA's undoing. President Barak Obama had just won his second term of office, and plans were being made for his upcoming presidential inauguration to be held on January 20th, 2013. As planning was underway, it was announced that the much celebrated pastor, Louie Giglio, had been invited to offer the benediction at the event. With the choice of Giglio, the White House had allied itself with a remarkably prominent Evangelical leader. His popularity among today's youth is self-evident, as seen through his multiple books and DVDs which have sold in the millions; his annual and highly attended *Passion Conference*; and his recording label, *Sixstepsrecords,* which is distributed by *Capitol Christian Music Group.* The magnitude of Giglio's cultural prominence made certain that many would be carefully watching his every move in association with the presidential inauguration: both friend and foe. All proceeded according to plan until an older sermon of Giglio's was discovered in which he called homosexuality a sin. With the full force of the internet at their disposal, those who made this find broadcasted their rage immediately, charging that such a view was incompatible for anyone who would be tasked to pray at the inaugural celebration. Amidst a time when the debate over homosexuality was swelling, this event seemed to capture the attention of the nation and well beyond. Giglio's past comments on homosexuality, delivered some fifteen years prior, were stirring important conversations about what the Bible actually says about marriage and sexuality. All of this seemed to produce the perfect storm of opportunity for Giglio to stand forth and state, boldly, what the Bible teaches on the subject of homosexuality, universal sin, and ultimately the Gospel of Jesus Christ. Sadly, what the waiting world received was something remarkably inferior. Shortly after the commotion over

Giglio was stirred, he announced his decision to resign: a choice that was encouraged by the White House,[125] but ultimately made by Giglio himself. He then published a letter to his church (Passion City Church) which was made available on the church's website and, as a result, the letter was more widely distributed to the public. In his letter, Giglio mentioned that, despite some ideological differences, he had fashioned a friendship with President Obama around the common goals of ending human trafficking. However, Giglio stated that he felt the necessity to withdraw his acceptance of the president's invitation to pray at the inauguration, and the reason he supplied for this choice was quite striking:

> "Neither I, nor our team, feel it best serves the core message and goals we are seeking to accomplish to be in a fight on an issue not of our choosing, thus I respectfully withdraw my acceptance of the President's invitation."

Nowhere in Giglio's resignation letter does he state or clarify what he actually believes it is that the Bible teaches on the subject of homosexuality. His silence on this matter, though largely unnoticed, was remarkably loud. For the benefit of those who had stirred this discussion, as well as those who follow his ministry, such a response would have provided a rich opportunity to address

---

[125]"We were not aware of Pastor Giglio's past comments at the time of his selection, and they don't reflect our desire to celebrate the strength and diversity of our country at this inaugural," said Addie Whisenant, the spokeswoman for the committee. "Pastor Giglio was asked to deliver the benediction in large part for his leadership in combating human trafficking around the world. As we now work to select someone to deliver the benediction, we will ensure their beliefs reflect this administration's vision of inclusion and acceptance for all Americans." NY Times *Minister Backs Out of Speech at Inaugural, Jan 10th* -
http://www.nytimes.com/2013/01/11/us/politics/minister-withdraws-from-inaugural-program-after-controversy-over-comments-on-gay-rights.html?_r=0

the realities of human sin, corruption, condemnation, and mankind's universal need for Christ. To date, Giglio has offered no statement of support, renunciation, or clarification regarding his one controversial message on homosexuality from the past.[126] His eagerness to avoid controversy was readily admitted in his resignation letter, where he said:

> "I'm confident that anyone who knows me or has listened to the multitude of messages I have given in the last decade would most likely conclude that I am not easily characterized as being opposed to people—any people. Rather, I am constantly seeking to understand where all people are coming from and how to best serve them as I point them to Jesus."

Giglio's thoughts regarding how others should perceive him are clearly a core concern of his, but should this really be the focus of a messenger of God? After all, the Apostles were riddled with faulty accusations throughout their respective ministries here on earth, but this never led them to flee from public contests. Even Christ Himself was accused of being a glutton and drunkard,[127] deceiver,[128] liar,[129] demoniac,[130] Sabbath breaker,[131] immoralist,[132] heretic,[133] and riot-maker;[134] yet our Savior unflinchingly declared truth to those who blasphemed Him. Exactly where in Scripture are believers enjoined to focus on the public's perception of them

---

[126] Prior to the writing of this book, I sought to gain clarification on his views regarding homosexuality by phone and private letter. To date, I have received no response from him, or any other leader from the church.

[127] Matthew 11:19a.

[128] John 7:12.

[129] Matthew 27:63.

[130] John 8:52.

[131] Luke 6:2.

[132] Luke 5:29-32, Matthew 11:19b.

[133] Matthew 26:65.

[134] Luke 23:14.

above the priority of proclaiming the truth? While the thought of pointing others to Jesus, as Giglio mentions, is commendable, we must wonder if this includes *the avoidance of opposing people – any people,* as he said. The dramatic reality all believers must face is that God's word is inherently divisive[135] in a Christ-hating world. Though this truth may seem harsh, we do ourselves and others no favors by pretending it is not real. Just the mere mention of biblical truth within this enmity-filled world is enough to provoke an abundance of hostility. Though we earnestly seek the reconciliation of the lost through the message of the Gospel,[136] we must also understand that the very Gospel which has the power to reconcile sinners to God is the same Gospel which divides, convicts, and cuts like a two edged sword.[137] Thus, to some, the knowledge of Christ is a sweet aroma. To others it is the stench of death:

> 2 Corinthians 2:14–17: 14 But thanks be to God, who always leads us in His triumph in Christ, and manifests through us the sweet aroma of the knowledge of Him in every place. 15 For we are a fragrance of Christ to God among those who are being saved and among those who are perishing; 16 to the one an aroma from death to death, to the other an aroma from life to life. And who is adequate for these things? 17 For we are not like many, peddling the word of God, but as from sincerity, but as from God, we speak in Christ in the sight of God.

While we must guard against the introduction of any offense due to our own sin or foolishness, we must never seek to nullify the

---

[135] Matthew 10:34-39.

[136] 2 Corinthians 5:20.

[137] Hebrews 4:12–13: 12 For the word of God is living and active and sharper than any two-edged sword, and piercing as far as the division of soul and spirit, of both joints and marrow, and able to judge the thoughts and intentions of the heart.13 And there is no creature hidden from His sight, but all things are open and laid bare to the eyes of Him with whom we have to do.

inherent offense of the Gospel. In the end, we cannot interfere with the manner in which the Spirit wields His own Sword,[138] for we have no governance over how men will respond to the truth when it is proclaimed. In his letter, Giglio rightly spoke of our nation's need for grace and mercy, however, one must wonder how he thought this should be achieved: "Our nation is deeply divided and hurting, and more than ever we need God's grace and mercy in our time of need." Giglio's expressed concern over America's deep divide and simultaneous need for grace and mercy raises further questions about his choice to resign and remain silent. Though conflict-avoidance may seem to issue such grace and mercy to this world, I must argue that it does not. As the pillar and support of the truth, the central means by which the church is to minister the love, grace, and mercy of Christ to this lost and dying world is by proclaiming God's word abroad. And while the subject of homosexuality is not the heart of the Gospel message by itself, *it is directly connected to it as is any sin.*[139] For this reason, the avoidance of this divisive subject is not the solution. If we faithfully and lovingly proclaim the truth of God's word, resulting in deep division and pain,[140] then we must accept this as a part of the Spirit's *promised ministry of convicting the world of sin, of righteousness, and of judgment.*[141]

I would submit to the reader that Giglio's reason for his withdrawal is deeply troubling. Before a watching world this highly celebrated pastor not only refrained from stating the Bible's clear teaching on homosexuality, but he also withdrew from any further debate or discourse on the subject altogether. Those who shouted loudly in support of the gay agenda successfully silenced a highly

---

[138] Ephesians 6:17.

[139] 1 Corinthians 6:9-11, Ephesians 5:5-6, Romans 1:18-32, Revelation 22:14-17.

[140] 1 Corinthians 1:18-23.

[141] John 16:7-11.

visible pastor on an issue that, in fact, *should be discussed for the sake of heralding Christ in the Gospel.* What became a victory for the homosexual community turned into a moment of shame for the church. Giglio's withdrawal from this controversy is also remarkable in view of a key statement he made in his Passion 2013 message, *Resurrecting These Bones,*

"No one does great things without going through fire."

His above statement is quite true, yet, we must wonder about the example he has set before a watching world. Those who follow this popular pastor may very well deduce from his example that it is best to avoid controversy, especially if the controversy in question is *not of one's own choosing - as Giglio said.* Yet, is this the example of the Apostles in the Scriptures? Is it not the case that the Apostle Paul was dragged into a great number of fights which were not of his choosing, and yet he embraced these conflicts as God's providential opportunities to proclaim the Gospel – both by word and deed? Paul rightly understood that the external conflicts which he experienced in this world only served the greater purpose of magnifying the name of Jesus in the message of Christ and Him crucified. Not counting his life as dear to himself, his principal priority was not self-preservation. Contrarily, if his priority had been that of self-preservation, or conflict avoidance, he would not have been able to finish the course of his ministry. As we observed the Apostle's words earlier: "I do not consider my life of any account as dear to myself, in order that I may finish my course, and the ministry which I received from the Lord Jesus, to testify solemnly of the gospel of the grace of God."[142] A simple reading of the book of Acts should remind us all that the sparks of conflict often spread the flames of the Gospel whenever the

---

[142] Acts 20:24.

Savior's Lordship is magnified over all aspects of life. In fact, it was precisely when Paul suffered as a prisoner in Philippi, singing praises to God from that musty cell of his, that his true emancipation in Christ was made evident to the Philippian jailer. The Philippian jailer knew that, though he was free, he was a slave to sin; and that though Paul was a prisoner, he was the true freedman of Christ (1 Cor. 7:22). When the watching world sees a Christian standing unflinchingly in the face of ungodly opposition, they are beholding a power that is truly supernatural. But when they see men fleeing contests in order to avoid unwanted controversy, or to appease men, they are seeing what all men do by their common, fallen nature. Flavel helps us on this very point:

> "...it is impossible to serve God without distractions, till we can serve him without the slavish fear of enemies."[143]

The example set by those who serve in leadership, for better or worse, is of critical importance. Pastors will either be the fearful slaves of men, or the slaves of Christ – the choice is simple, but quite grave. They will either preach the whole counsel of God for the glory of the Master (Acts 20:27), or cherry pick messages which satisfy the expectations of this world. Should a pastor find himself among that latter category, he will have the shameful bloodguilt of men on his hands. All believers must face down the common temptation of thinking that by gaining some measure of leverage with the world, the church can minister more effectively; instead, the ultimate result is that the fulcrum of worldly evil eventually brings Christ's body down.

As we think further about the growing conflict over the subject of homosexuality in our nation, the church should consider what her

---

[143] Flavel, <u>A Practical Treatise of Fear</u>, 271.

approach to this ought to be. The culture in which we live will most certainly demand that we address this subject as time continues. Homosexual sin, like any other sin, is an opportunity to explain a universal truth about all mankind:

> John 8:34: Jesus answered them, "Truly, truly, I say to you, everyone who commits sin is the slave of sin."

This is the subject of slavery that should capture our attention the most, especially when we consider mankind's greatest need. As the Savior teaches, *all are slaves of sin, because all men sin.* The good news of the Gospel is that though the natural man is a slave of sin, he can be emancipated by the One who has all power over sin and death:[144]

> John 8:36: "If therefore the Son shall make you free, you shall be free indeed."

One of Satan's great tactics is to have men believe that they are truly free when, in reality, they are not. Much of what is so offensive about the Gospel is that its message is just the opposite of Satan's deception. Thus, the Gospel stands as an offense to the earthly and carnal desires of lost men, but if we love the lost *truly*, we should share the *truth* with them for the glory of Christ no matter what the results may be. Shrinking back from this priority is not an option for the disciples of Christ. Imagine if one were to redact the book of Acts such that every contest which Paul faced, *not of his choosing*, ended with his preemptive flight from such controversies. Such an approach to conflict would have resulted in the stifling of his preaching and exemplification of the grace of God[145] in the presence of men. Of course, he would have been

---

[144] 1 Corinthians 15:57.
[145] 1 Thessalonians 1:5-13.

spared from the "beatings, imprisonments, and tumults" (2 Corinthians 6:5), the very afflictions which gave his physical appearance the mutilating *brand-marks of Jesus.* (Gal 6:17). Yet, neither would he have carried the fragrant aroma of Christ as one who could say: "...indeed, we had the sentence of death within ourselves so that we would not trust in ourselves, but in God who raises the dead" (2 Cor 1:9). In all of this, I am greatly concerned that the modern culture of Christendom is more caught up with mere form and fashion than it is with the brutal realities of a life that is fully dedicated to the Gospel ministry. It would appear that men today are more preoccupied with cool appearances, hipster haircuts, and whatever else is deemed as trendy within this world. As Spurgeon once said, "...we need soldiers, not fops,[146] earnest laborers, not genteel loiterers."[147] Simply put, any shepherd who wishes to emulate the Good Shepherd in this harsh battle of life must remember that it is not an option to flee at the sight of encroaching wolves. The habit of hirelings has no place in public ministry:

John 10:12–13: 12 "He who is a hireling, and not a shepherd, who is not the owner of the sheep, beholds the wolf coming, and leaves the sheep, and flees, and the wolf snatches them, and scatters them.13 "He flees because he is a hireling, and is not concerned about the sheep."

The watching world does not need more silence from the church, instead it needs brethren to speak the truth in love, even though that truth may be hated with satanic fervor. As already noted, the debate over homosexuality is not a distraction from the Gospel. The relevancy of the doctrine of marriage and the doctrine of universal sin points to the Lord's plan of redemption. There is,

---

[146] Fop: A man who is excessively concerned with his appearance.

[147] C.H. Spurgeon, Lectures to My Students, (Grand Rapids: Zoncervan Publishing, 1996), 36.

however, another point of connection between the homosexual debate and the Bible. In God's divine providence it is profoundly ironic that the homosexual community's banner of choice is, of all things, *the rainbow*.[148] I call this ironic in view of God's purpose for the rainbow, as juxtaposed to the homosexual community's maligned use of it. When we consider the rainbow's origin, we find a remarkable message of God's judgment and mercy with respect to mankind. Having destroyed the world of wickedness in a deluge, God gave Noah the promise that He would never again destroy all flesh by means of a flood. Therefore God revealed to Noah "the bow [*hăqqeśeṯ*] that is in the cloud" (i.e., rain*bow*) as His symbol to all of mankind that He would refrain from giving humanity what it otherwise deserves, thereby supplying a measure of mercy to the sons of men while they live on the earth. The Hebrew word *hăqqeśeṯ* is normally used in reference to a bow used in hunting or warfare. Those who have ever drawn a recurve bow know that it takes an abundance of strength to draw and sustain a bow's tension. Releasing the bow is the easy part, but keeping it drawn and restrained for long periods of time requires significant force. I would suggest to the reader that this very concept represents two important truths: *1. God is mercifully withholding the wrath that we deserve due to indwelling sin; and 2. One day, His bow of wrath will be released in the judgment of men.* It is this very picture of God's temporal mercy upon the sons of men that is similarly unveiled in the New Testament: "He who believes in the Son has eternal life; but he who does not obey the Son will not see life, *but the wrath of God abides on him.*" (John 3:36). This text in John 3

---

[148] The establishment of the rainbow, as a symbol for the homosexual community, is normally attributed to Gilbert Baker – an artist from San Francisco – who first designed the flag in 1978. There is no apparent evidence that Baker was attempting to imitate the Bible's description of the rainbow in Genesis 9. Instead, the homosexual community has used several colors (in recent history) in order to depict various aspects and perspectives of the gay community.

unpacks some of the inherent symbolism of God's *hăqqeśet* (bow) of judgment and mercy: His mercy is now active such that men "live and move and exist" (Acts 17:28), enjoying "rains and fruitful seasons" here on the earth (Acts 14:17). Yet, John 3:36 tells us that God's wrath "abides" on all those who do not obey the Son. That word "abides" (*menei*) is a present active indicative verb, indicating a present and ongoing reality in God's relation with this world. John 3:36 is a picture of presently restrained wrath denoting an active tension of God's present mercy which will someday give way to the release of His just and eternal wrath upon all those who resist Him. In the days of Noah, the world of sinful men was destroyed by water, but in His final judgment the present heavens and earth will be destroyed by fire such that even the elements will be consumed with intense heat.[149]   In all of this, the rainbow is both awesomely beautiful, yet haunting in light of its implied message. Overall, the rainbow is not just a fearful warning to the homosexual community, it is a fearful declaration to all men in light of God's promised future wrath. It is a reminder that all have sinned and fall short of God's glory (Romans 3:23); and that the wages of our sin is death (Romans 6:23); therefore, apart from Christ, all men are counted as God's enemies (Romans 5:8) and must plead for mercy and grace which is fully revealed in His Son, Jesus Christ. Like the discussion of marriage, it is impossible to discuss the sin of homosexuality without discussing the Gospel and our universal need for Christ.

If possible, as far as it depends upon us, we are to be at peace with all men,[150] yet without a shred of compromise over truth. Any peace that is achieved at the expense of heralding God's truth and

---

[149] 2 Peter 3:3-10.

[150] Romans 12:18: 18 If possible, so far as it depends on you, be at peace with all men.

glory is no peace at all. Much precious blood has been spilled throughout history by saints who refused to shrink back from upholding God's word in a fallen world, and for this reason we can echo the truth that *the blood of the martyrs is the seed of the church.*[151] It would be a dangerous presumption to conclude that the persecutions of yesteryear could never revisit the church again. Flavel warned his readers of such a dangerous presumption, especially in view of those brethren throughout history who suffered and died in the defense of God's truth:

"We are conscious to ourselves how far short we come in holiness, innocency, and spiritual excellency of those excellent persons who have suffered these things; and therefore have no ground to expect more favour from providence than they found...If we think these evils shall not come in our days, it is like many of them thought so too; and yet they did, and we may find it quite otherwise (Lam. iv. 12)...the same race and kind of men that committed these outrages upon our brethren, are still in being...their rage and malice is not abated in the least degree, but is as fierce and cruel as ever it was..."[152]

The Lord promises His people many things in His word, one of which is the promise given by the Apostle Paul: *all who desire to live godly in Christ Jesus will be persecuted.*[153] When affliction arises, we may be tempted to flee in the face of opposition, but we must resist this in reverence for Christ. John Bunyan did not write *The Pilgrim's Progress* in the quietude and comfort of his pastor's study; instead, he wrote it while serving time in jail. His "crime" was quite simple: as a non-conformist minister, he refused to stop preaching the Gospel of Jesus Christ, and for this he was imprisoned twice for a total of thirteen years. Had Bunyan wished

---

[151] Normally attributed to Tertullian.

[152] Flavel, <u>A Practical Treatise of Fear</u>, p. 267.

[153] 2 Timothy 3:12.

to avoid this conflict, all that was required was his silence, but this was an idolatrous sacrifice that he refused to offer up to his earthly overlords. Instead, Bunyan retained his witness for Christ and the Gospel by refusing to seek the approval and praise of the men of this world. Understanding the corruption of seeking worldly praise and affirmation, Bunyan created the obsequious character, Mr. By-ends, who was from the land of Fair-speech. His love for worldly praise belied his professed love for Christ. Christian asked Mr. By-ends who his relatives were in the town of Fair-speech, and this was his response:

> "Almost the whole town; and in particular my Lord Turn-about, my Lord Time-server, my Lord Fair-speech, from whose ancestors that town first took its name; also, Mr. Smooth-man, Mr. Facing-both-ways, Mr. Any-thing; and the parson of our parish, Mr. Two-tongues, was my mother's own brother, by father's side...'Tis true, we somewhat differ in religion from those of the stricter sort, yet but in two small points: First, we never strive against wind and tide. Secondly, we are always most zealous when religion goes in his silver slippers; we love much to walk with him in the street, if the sun shines and the people applaud him."[154]

When we honestly and openly admit our imperfection and frailty as mere men, we must admit that the hypocrisy of Mr. By-ends and his kin is much closer to us all than we might wish to believe. Only by God's grace we can resist such compromise by living as lights in this dark world.

---

[154] John Bunyan, *The Pilgrim's Progress.*

MY BANNER IS CHRIST

~ CHAPTER VII ~

SOLUS CHRISTUS

IN THE HOME

AND CHURCH

As our nation continues to descend to a level of depravity comparable to that of Sodom and Gomorrah, Christ's body must resolve to stand firm in the strength of His might knowing that the true warfare we face is not physical, but spiritual: *For our struggle is not against flesh and blood, but against the rulers, against the powers, against the world forces of this darkness, against the spiritual forces of wickedness in the heavenly places* (Ephesians 6:12). Equipped with the full armour of our God (Ephesians 6:13-18), we must face the foes of Christ rather than flee from their presence. We must also be warned about that deceitful spirit *which is most zealous when religion goes in his silver slippers, if the sun shines, and the people applaud us.* Flavel underscores this important lesson for us very well:

> "As long as we can profess religion without any great hazard of life, liberty, or estates, we may show much zeal and forwardness in the ways of godliness: but when it comes to the sharps, to *resisting unto blood*, few will be found to own and assert it openly in the face of such dangers. The first retreat is usually made from a free and open, to a close and concealed practice of religion; not opening our windows, as Daniel did, to shew we care not who knows we dare worship our God, and are not ashamed of our duties, but hiding our principles and practice with all the art and care imaginable, reckoning it well if we can escape danger by letting fall our profession which might expose us to it..."[155]

Clearly, the fear of man is a dangerous disease to the soul. Yet, the believer who serves in the fear of Christ will forsake all such ungodly fear, while boldly advancing the Gospel of peace no matter what consequences may come. Such boldness comes not from the flesh, but from the Holy Spirit who enables us to stand firm on the front line of battle rather than retreat in fear.

---

[155] Flavel, <u>A Practical Treatise of Fear</u>, p. 277.

Whatever else prominent men may be found doing, Christ's body must be readied for battle with all sobriety and readiness, and this readiness begins with the individual's pursuit of spiritual growth and maturation. Those who are tasked with leadership in the church and home must shepherd those under their care in view of the enemy's never-ending assault on God's people. They must remember that our interaction with the world does not consist of a friendly social,[156] it instead consists of a very grave, spiritual warfare. Fearful times demand fearless servants and soldiers, and it is for this reason that all of God's people must remember that our Commander in Chief goes before us with His immutable victory over sin and death. We can do all things through Christ who strengthens us. Apart from Him, we will most certainly fall.

One day during my early seminary years I was given yet another reminder of the spiritual battle that we face, not only in the world but within our own souls. While traveling home after a long day of studies, I stopped by my favorite bookstore in order to search for some inexpensive treasures in the shop's $1 or less closeout book-bin. In little time I came across a vaguely familiar title which had been quite popular in the previous decade and had been recommended to me by a number of friends over the years. In the past, this book had been of no interest to me seeing that it appeared to be yet another prescription for seeker sensitive thinking. However, now that I was holding the title at the closeout price of less than a dollar, I decided to pick it up out of curiosity. As I examined it further, my rather ordinary find became somewhat extraordinary when I discovered that the book had been signed by the author himself, and his autograph was underscored with a reference to Philippians 2:13. However, juxtaposed to his signature was a newspaper clipping on the opposite page,

---

[156] James 4:4.

consisting of no more than two short paragraphs. Under the heading, "Adultery," the article issued a clinical description of the famous author's resignation from pastoral ministry as the result of an eight year adulterous affair. I was saddened by my discovery, but not at all surprised. I say this because what is perhaps more striking than the story of this book and its famous author is the fact that there are many other such stories to recall. Even during the writing of this book, two highly celebrated pastors within the Reformed community resigned their pastorates due to adultery, with one of them being restored to ministry two months later. Another significant pastoral failure, due to adultery, took place in 2013 and hit many churches like a ton of bricks. This pastor had been highly acclaimed for his teachings on the subjects of marriage and family. I first heard of this man in 2004 when multiple families excitedly sought my affirmation of his books, sermons, seminars, and parachurch ministry. However, after perusing one of his more popular works, I felt strongly disinclined to offer any public support of this man. As in many other cases I have experienced, my concern wasn't that rank heresy was being promoted. Instead, what this man had written fell short in its scriptural exposition and emphasis on the centrality of Christ. I wasn't interested in condemning the man and his ministry; I just didn't want to become one of his advocates. Thus, as I have experienced so many times before and since, my unwillingness to join the promotional parade of yet another rising Evangelical star led to the great disappointment of a number of individuals in our church. In the end, experiences like these draw attention away from the church's central priorities of *Solus Christus* and *Sola Scriptura* and, they are, unfortunately, all too common. However, modern Evangelicalism's insatiable appetite for men of prominence would be well mortified if its members would recall the demise of Korah and his *250 men of renown*.[157] To be sure, the mass grave of those men, memorialized by the Lord,[158] testifies to God's people of all ages that *reverence for social prominence* is a lethal idol. The important lesson which stands for Christ's body is this: the life and health of the church does not depend upon the rise or fall of prominent men, it depends on the exalted and risen Lord and Savior, Jesus Christ. Yet, this important lesson is too often ignored amidst the hot pursuit Evangelicalism's rising stars, and all of this has proven to be exhausting and destructive to Christ's body. The church is not to be an idol-seeking talent show, searching for the next batch of preachers who can wow the masses with a fresh wave of books, videos, and conferences. Instead, pastors in the local church have a very *simple* and *pure* calling: to magnify one person, the Lord Jesus Christ and to deliver His word to His sheep and to this lost world. What I find so alarming is the ease with which individuals are so easily taken in by the modern under-currents of celebritism. The form and appearance of a man in the ministry can often look very commendable at a distance, but his true nature is best seen up close and in person – *over time*. Thus, the preacher seen on a video screen may be very impressive for his oration, elocution, and demonstrated knowledge, but if he is not present *among the people* (1 Peter 5:2) as one who is *becoming an example to the flock* before their eyes (1 Peter 5:3), then he is nothing more than a well-spoken stranger. The Apostle Peter helps us to consider the importance of a pastor's need to develop and grow in the presence of a watching flock:

---

[157] Numbers 16:1-33.

[158] Numbers 16:38: 38 "As for the censers of these men who have sinned at the cost of their lives, let them be made into hammered sheets for a plating of the altar, since they did present them before the LORD and they are holy; and they shall be for a sign to the sons of Israel."

1 Peter 5:1–4: 1 THEREFORE, I exhort the elders among you, as your fellow elder and witness of the sufferings of Christ, and a partaker also of the glory that is to be revealed, 2 shepherd the flock of God among you, exercising oversight not under compulsion, but voluntarily, according to the will of God; and not for sordid gain, but with eagerness; 3 nor yet as lording it over those allotted to your charge, but *proving to be examples to the flock.* 4 And when the Chief Shepherd appears, you will receive the unfading crown of glory. (italics mine)

The expression, *proving to be examples to the flock,* is derived from the Greek: *tupoi ginomenoi,* literally meaning – *becoming examples.* Peter's use of the present participle *ginomenoi* [*becoming*] speaks of the overseer's perpetual transformation born out in the sight of the church.[159] The picture employed here is not static, but dynamic and ongoing, like a motion picture. Thus, Peter reminds elders and the church that those who serve as overseers are imperfect men who will continue to grow in their servitude of the Chief Shepherd. When reading the Gospels, we are often reminded of Peter's own sin and frailty, especially when he denied the Savior three times out of his fear of men. Yet, the Peter of 1 Peter 5 was clearly a new man who came to understand the importance of looking to the Chief Shepherd with reverence and undistracted longing. Over time, Peter had matured so as to become an example to the flock himself, and all of this heralded the powerful grace of God.

1 Peter 5:1-4 reminds us that the biblical model of leadership is one that calls for an interaction between shepherds and sheep that is close and personal. It is in this context that a man can be known, not just for what he says, but also for his life which is constantly being transformed by God's grace. However, this scriptural model is often replaced with a business model where pastors operate

---

[159] G. *ginomenoi* – present active participle of *ginomai* (be, become).

more like CEOs who are managing a corporation. The contemporary model of mega-churches, satellite campuses, livestreamed preaching, and internet-based ministry has, in too many cases, served to replace the scriptural model of personal and direct interaction between under-shepherds and their sheep. An environment like this often creates a kind of professional distance between leaders and the congregation, while the people conduct themselves like the employees of a company. As a result, biblical accountability is weakened within the church and, those households that are influenced by such thinking tend to demote, rather than promote, the father's relational leadership of his family. Any such model like this, whatever the size, is an affront to what Christ ordained for His church. In the end, all of this generates an environment and attitude which yields a dangerous vacuum of accountability for everyone involved. Yet the standard of Scripture is remarkably different than the CEO-pastoral-celebrity culture of the modern church:

1 Timothy 3:1–7: 1 IT is a trustworthy statement: if any man aspires to the office of overseer, it is a fine work he desires to do. 2 An overseer, then, must be above reproach, the husband of one wife, temperate, prudent, respectable, hospitable, able to teach, 3 not addicted to wine or pugnacious, but gentle, uncontentious, free from the love of money. 4 He must be one who manages his own household well, keeping his children under control with all dignity 5 (but if a man does not know how to manage his own household, how will he take care of the church of God?); 6 and not a new convert, lest he become conceited and fall into the condemnation incurred by the devil. 7 And he must have a good reputation with those outside the church, so that he may not fall into reproach and the snare of the devil.

Paul delivered these qualifications to Timothy so that it would be understood that, in order for Christ and His authority to be magnified in the church,[160] those who serve in leadership must have certain non-negotiable qualities *that can be seen and verified.* Of the many he lists, Paul's mention of a man's ministry in the home is quite striking. By this qualification alone, Paul established this unimpeachable standard: if a man is to shepherd a church then he must first be a shepherd in his own home. When we consider Paul's important correspondence between the home and the church, many powerful implications come forth that have been diminished in the modern era. One such implication is that the pastor's life should serve as a visible model for all husbands and fathers in Christ's body. If a pastor conducts himself like a distant CEO in the church, this mentality can impact his household as well as the households of other men who seek to imitate his example. Moreover, if a pastor is not a minister of the Gospel, leader, and instructor in his own household, then his bad influence will also spread to other men and families like gangrene. In the end, a man's conduct amidst his family is the crucible in which his true metal is tested and known, as Bunyan has observed in his classic work, *Family Duty*:

> "He that is the master of a family, he hath, as under that relation, a work to do for God; to wit, the right governing of his own family...Further, we find also in the New Testament, that they are looked upon as Christians of an inferior rank that have not a due regard to this duty; yea, so inferior as not fit to be chosen to any office in the church of God."[161]

Bunyan's words remind us of the foundational importance of a man's spiritual leadership in the home. The Puritans frequently

---

[160] 1 Timothy 3:15.

[161] John Bunyan, *Family Duty*, (Pensacola: Chapel Library),
http://www.chapellibrary.org/files/8513/7643/3202/fdut.pdf, (accessed June 22nd, 2015).

used the expression, *family duties*, in reference to the priority of a husband and father leading and managing his household under Christ's authority. This reflects one of the key legacies of the Puritans and the Reformers: they restored the primacy of God's word in the church and in individual households. With such a regained emphasis on *Sola Scriptura*, along with the understanding that all believers are able to read and understand Holy Writ by the leading of the Holy Spirit, the church moved beyond Rome's spiritual bondage and darkness. Men rediscovered the importance of God's call in their lives to lead their households by means of the authority of God's word (Ephesians 5:22-33) and to bring up their children in the discipline and instruction of the Lord (Ephesians 6:4). J.W. Alexander well summarizes the shepherding responsibilities of all men who serve Christ as husbands and fathers:

"The hour of domestic prayer and praise is also the hour of scriptural instruction. The father has opened God's Word, in the presence of his little flock. He thus admits himself to be its teacher and under-shepherd. The example of a father is acknowledged to be all-important. The stream must not be expected to rise higher than the fountain. The Christian householder will feel himself constrained to say: 'I am leading my family in solemn addresses to God; what manner of man should I be! How wise, holy, and exemplary!' This undoubtedly has been, in cases innumerable, the direct operation of Family-Worship on the father. As we know that worldly men, and inconsistent professors, are deterred from performing this duty by the consciousness of a discrepancy between their life and any acts of devotion, so humble Christians are led by the same comparison to be more circumspect, and to order their ways in such a manner as may edify their dependents. There cannot be too many motives to a holy life, nor too many safeguards to parental example. Establish the worship of God in any house, and you erect around it a new barrier against the irruption of the world, the flesh, and the devil."[162]

There is great safety within a home which seeks to exalt Christ and His word. For the father, there is a great accountability which comes with his pulpit in the home. His ministry to his wife and children is a serious one, requiring prayer and diligence on his part. There is also great safety for the family that receives such leadership, just as a small flock does when following the lead of a careful shepherd. Sadly, the scriptural wisdom espoused by men like Bunyan, J.W. Alexander, and many others has been buried beneath decades of compromise, neglect, and unscriptural teaching. The space required to cover this important subject of family duty within the church exceeds the scope of this chapter and it is for this reason that I have incorporated a section entitled, *The Fear of Christ in Marriage and Family,* in the second appendix of this book. There, I address what the church must recover in any generation: a high regard for marriage (Ephesians 5:22-33) and family (Ephesians 6:1-4) *all of which flows from a subjection and servitude in the fear of Christ* (Ephesians 5:21). The contents of the second appendix are as follows: *1. The Fear of Christ in the First Institution of Marriage; 2. The Fear of Christ in the Husband; 3. The Fear of Christ in the Wife; and 4. The Fear of Christ in the Home.* This review of marriage and family was made as an appendix, not because it is less significant, but because of its length and distinct focus of study. For this reason, I strongly advise the reader to consult that section as a crucial aid to this chapter. Overall, it has been my concern for many years that the ministry of the word in the home has suffered a serious and dangerous

---

[162] James W. Alexander, Thoughts on Family Worship (Morgan PA: Soli Deo Gloria Publications), 49-50.

downgrade. With the continued onslaught of *effeminism*,[163] feminism, the emasculation of men, rampant divorce, the mutilation of marriage, and indifference towards children in the home, it should be no surprise that we now live in a world of madness where little children are being taught to question their gender identities at very young ages. Sadly, many of these aforementioned influences have crept into the church in ways that too few have noticed. Because of this, many Christians have developed a remarkable illiteracy concerning the Scripture's teaching on the roles of men and women along with the leadership role of the father in the home. When people recoil at Scriptural language regarding a husband's headship and management of his home, or of the wife's calling to submit to such leadership, they reveal just how much of the world is now in the professing church.

All of this brings to mind the importance of Paul's list of qualifications for overseers in the church. Churches are often eager to seek a pastor who is *apt to teach*, but in this modern era there seems to be less concern about his pulpit in the home. A disconnect like this is poisonous to the leadership of the church and to all those under their influence. What the church must remember is that genuine overseers are not created by manmade programs, institutions, or standards; rather, it is God who sovereignly calls overseers such that their conduct and character will become evident before a watching church, in God's time. Such a process as this reminds God's people that it is God who builds His church, not men, and that those who will eventually be called to serve as overseers will continue to be in public what they are in the private. When leaders live this way in the presence of the

---

[163] Please see Appendix II, *The Fear of Christ in Marriage and Family*, for a more detailed description of the problems of effeminism and feminism.

people, they promote and encourage the same healthy habits needed in every household:

1. A Man's *Focus* of Leadership: According to what Paul teaches in 1 Timothy 3:4, a godly man manages *his own household* [*idiou oikou*] well. This statement clarifies for us the fact that a man's own household is his *foremost responsibility.* Should he fail here, he reveals to all what Bunyan called a character of "inferior rank." Thus, a man's *own family* is the veritable canary in the coal mine signifying either spiritual health or illness. This is true for all men, especially for those who aspire to the office of overseer: an office that is designed to set forth a godly example to the flock. When overseers treat their own households as their foremost responsibility, other heads of households are buttressed in a priority that is universal for all husbands and fathers. It is for this reason that overseers must pass this qualification, otherwise they will spread the germ of an inferior and dangerous priority.

2. The *Nature* of a Man's Leadership: Paul reminds us that men are called to *manage* their households *well.* The word manage [*proistamenon*] literally means "standing before others," denoting a clear and decisive leadership/management. This concept is important and harmonizes well with Ephesians 5:23, where all husbands are commanded to lead their homes because the husband is the "head of the wife, as Christ also is the head of the church." It is here that Paul reminds husbands and fathers that their core priority is to herald, magnify, and imitate Christ for the sake of their wives and children through a Christ-centered leadership. Such truths as these obliterate the contemporary mythology of co-leadership between husbands and wives in the home. A modern trend among churches today is to have women serving in leadership roles next to or in place of men with the ever increasing popularity of husband and wife pastoral teams. Though these ecclesiastical choices are increasing in demand, they send dangerous ripples throughout the church while spreading an abundance of confusion regarding the roles of men and women. Such practices nullify Paul's calling for *men* to serve as overseers who *manage their households well.* In a home which upholds Christ's authority, the wife is the helper to her husband according to the creation ordinance (Genesis 2:18), but not a co-leader (Ephesians 5:22-6:4, 1 Timothy 2:9-15). Decades of effeminism and feminism in the world have influenced the modern church in such a way that these principles are frequently undermined, and, because of this, men are often fearful of leading their homes in view of such secular pressures. However, a man who loves his wife truly is the one who, in the imitation of Christ, will supply a decisive leadership which provides a haven of protection for her and the children. As an example of this principle of loving leadership, God's covenant of grace with Abraham reveals an important kernel of truth: "For I have chosen him, so that he may command [H. *yātzwe*] his children and his household after him to keep the way of the LORD by doing righteousness and justice, so that the LORD may bring upon Abraham what He has spoken about him." Genesis 18:19. This command given to Abraham comes from the root word *mitzwā* (commandment) and is correctly translated as "command" in the NASB. Whatever else the reader might think or assume about the nature of Abraham's calling of leadership, it was rooted in a clear and decisive management based upon the "way of the Lord." Abraham was not called to delegate this responsibility to others; nor was he allowed to neglect it or relegate it to his wife Sarah; instead, it was Abraham's responsibility before God alone. In the end, if a man does not lead his household in this manner, he is shirking his duty before God.

3. The *Pedagogy* of a Man's Leadership: According to Scripture, a godly husband must seek the sanctification of his wife (Ephesians 5:25-33) and his children (Ephesians 6:4) by means of the ministry of the word. This principle establishes the importance of regular worship in the home (i.e., "family duties" - devotions/worship). However, spiritual indifference leads men to the neglect of such duties, but love for Christ drives a man to such privileges with great joy. In homes where such a pedagogy of love takes place, one will find the fruit of peace and joy. However, wherever such a pedagogy is weak or absent, uncertainty, sorrow, fear, depression, anxiety, discontentment, provocation, and anger will fester and grow.[164] It is in this sense that every husband and father must labor as a shepherd in his own household, leading by the authority of God's word, while heralding Christ's supreme authority in everything. This ministry of the word fosters a deeper love, adoration, and reverence for Christ. Though a man may never preach in a pulpit of the church, the pulpit of his home still remains his responsibility before God. This is why such leadership in the home is seen as the primitive pre-requisite for the overseer. It is for this reason that the under-shepherd must manifest this important duty of family worship for the sake of his own household as well as for the sake of other men who will watch and imitate his example. Simply put, a man is not *apt to teach* if he is not leading and teaching his wife and children in the home first and foremost.

4. The *Ministerial Openness* of a Man's Home: Paul's mention of *hospitality* in 1 Timothy 3:2 must not be seen as a mere expression of social etiquette, instead it has to do with the quality of loving those who are outside of one's household.[165] It is in this sense that hospitality is the believer's opportunity to give expression to the foremost commandment by loving God *and loving one's neighbor.*[166] Such openness and generosity should be common among all brethren,[167] but it should especially be modelled by the man who would be an overseer. If an overseer does not model this before Christ's sheep, then hospitality will wane throughout the church. Additionally, hospitality is important because it supplies a means by which the shepherd can interact with, and be visible before, others within the church. Paul's instruction about hospitality should bring to mind Peter's important command in 1 Peter 5:2-3: "[shepherd the flock of God among you...] nor yet as lording it over those allotted to your charge, but *proving to be*

---

[164] Ephesians 6:4.

[165] Such a ministry should be extended to other brethren as well as to others in his broader community: "So then, while we have opportunity, let us do good to all men, and especially to those who are of the household of the faith." Galatians 6:10.

[166] Mark 12:28-31.

[167] Acts 2:44-45, Romans 12:13.

examples to the flock." Thus, a pastor is not a fixed, motionless statue, but is a living, breathing human being who is being transformed by the power of God's grace such that his life is one that is becoming a greater example to the people who watch him. Despite his flaws as a human being, he, his wife, and children are all growing in wisdom and grace – and the open act of hospitality avails such progress to a church that is called to emulate such an example. Again, hospitality is more than social etiquette – it is the ministry through which sheep can see and imitate their shepherd and his family in a very real way.

5. The Centrality of *Love* in Everything: Interestingly, 1 Timothy 3:1-7 is devoid of any explicit mention of love; however, the notion of love is implicitly revealed in every qualification. *First*, I say this because, as the foremost commandment is indeed *foremost* in every dimension of life (Deuteronomy 6:4-5, Mark 12:28-31), no aspect of the believer's life should be untouched by such love. *Second*, Paul's description of the nature of love in 1 Corinthians 13:1-7 reveals several parallels of thought when compared to 1 Timothy 3:1-7. Additionally, as we have already considered, a man's leadership in his home must reflect that of Christ's loving leadership of the church: "Husbands, love your wives, just as Christ also loved the church and gave Himself up for her..." (Ephesians 5:25). Thus, a man's loving devotion and fidelity towards his wife is the first test for his fidelity towards other responsibilities in life. This foundation of love is for all men, and it is the foundation which must stand firmly in the life of an overseer.

6. The *Universal Standards* of Leadership: As a final point of observation, Paul's list of qualifications in 1 Timothy 3:1-7 are delivered without a single shred of human prejudice. At no point in time does he issue points of negotiation on any given standard of piety. If leaders ever seek to change, modulate, or compromise on these standards, then they establish a banner of man-centered hypocrisy before a watching church. Unfortunately, it is sometimes the case that churches will fall into the temptation of fudging the standards of pastoral leadership for the sake of giving preference to certain individuals. For instance, if a man is highly educated and credentialed, he may be called to serve in leadership despite other apparent flaws. Or a church may look to call a man who is popular among the people, though his marriage and family may be weak. This can also happen if a man is a prominent business leader, highly respected member of the community, or an articulate teacher. Sometimes churches establish differentiated expectations between "staff" and "non-staff" overseers, despite the fact that Paul offers no such modulation of the biblical standards. Though all men will vary in their giftedness before God, no man who seeks to serve in leadership can fall short of the baseline of qualifications in 1 Timothy 3:1-7. Though it is recognized that those elders who are primarily focused on public preaching and teaching are to be mindful of James' warnings concerning teachers (James 3:1), such a notion in no way mitigates the biblical qualifications for "non-staff" elders. Elders who frequent the pulpit as well as those who do not should all be invested in pursuing the elder qualifications stipulated in 1 Timothy 3:1-7, Titus 1:5-9, and 1 Peter 5:1-4 - because none of these texts establish any distinction among those who teach frequently versus those who teach with less frequency. The standards for overseers are not just for those with a seminary degree, or for those who readily fill the pulpit, but they apply to all who bear the title and office of overseer; and a conscientious pastor should seek the application of these standards among all leaders within the church so that he might be surrounded with the kind of accountability that he truly needs for the sake of his life, his doctrine, and his example before Christ's sheep. The removal or avoidance of these standards is spiritually dangerous to the pastor and the entire church.

Under-shepherds who serve Christ well in the home will serve and lead the church with honor and integrity, and will supply a much-needed example for all husbands and fathers. Bunyan was right to observe that "they are looked upon as Christians of an inferior rank that have not a due regard to this duty [family duty]; yea, so inferior as not fit to be chosen to any office in the church of God." This is why 1 Timothy 3:1-7 should be seen, not only as the qualifications of an elder, *but also as the model of godliness for all men in Christ's body.* In view of this need for godly examples in the church, the overseer must be able to do more than wax eloquent on theology, he must be a man who is *becoming an example before the flock of God.* The future progeny of leadership in the church requires such examples from qualified men, but when a church is bankrupt of such examples, whole households and the entire flock will suffer. It is in this vein of thought that Thomas Manton issued his concerns in his foreword to the Westminster Confession of Faith:

"I CANNOT suppose thee to be such a stranger in England as to be ignorant of the general complaint concerning the decay of the power of godliness, and more especially of the great corruption of youth. Wherever thou goest, thou wilt hear men crying out of bad children and bad servants; whereas indeed the source of the mischief must be sought a little higher: it is bad parents and bad masters that make bad children and bad servants; and we cannot blame so much their untowardness, as our own negligence in their education. The devil hath a great spite at the kingdom of Christ, and he knoweth no such compendious way to crush it in the egg, as by the perversion of youth, and supplanting family-duties. He striketh at all those duties which are publick in the assemblies of the saints; but these are too well guarded by the solemn injunctions and dying charge of Jesus Christ, as that he should ever hope totally to subvert and undermine them; but at family duties he striketh with the more success because the institution is not so solemn, and the practice not so seriously and conscientiously regarded as it should be, and the omission is not so liable to notice and public censure...now, the devil knoweth that this is a blow at the root, and a ready way to prevent the succession of Churches: if he can subvert families, other societies and communities will not long flourish and subsist with any power and vigor; for there is the stock from whence they are supplied both for the present and future. For the present: A family is the seminary of Church and State; and if children be not well principled there, all miscarrieth: a fault in the first concoction is not mended in the second; if youth be bred ill in the family, they prove ill in Church and Commonwealth; there is the first making or marring, and the presage of their future lives to be thence taken, Prov. 20:11. By family discipline, officers are trained up for the Church, 1 Tim. 3:4..."[168]

Manton, and other Puritans like him, strongly emphasized the importance of *family duties* (or *family discipleship*) – an emphasis which we greatly need in the modern era. If Christ is to be exalted in His church, this must take place at all levels of the body, from the leadership to the pew. In every household, the father must seek to uphold the priorities of *Solus Christus* and *Sola Scriptura* rather than expecting others to do this as his substitute. Scripture is clear regarding the father's responsibilities before God:

Ephesians 6:4: And, fathers, do not provoke your children to anger; but bring them up in the discipline and instruction of the Lord.

When fathers embrace their calling to nurture, lead, and teach in the home, with the help and encouragement of their wives, they fulfill their calling before God to be the shepherds of their households. When families are thus lead, then they become what Manton calls the "seminary of Church and State." However, when men fail to lead in this manner, they expose themselves and their families to Satan's agenda. This is why churches need something other than video-streamed mega-pastors who remain strangers to the average man in the pew. Instead, Christ's body needs under-shepherds who lead in their homes well, thereby providing a much needed model for all men who are to be the shepherds in their homes. Pastors who encourage such growth among the men of the church will find themselves surrounded with the kind of spiritual accountability that they themselves need and ought to desire.

---

[168] This excerpt from Thomas Manton's, *Epistle to the Reader*, is presented in complete form in the third appendix.

Overall, God's design for His church is to have all men serving as leaders, by word *and deed*, beneath the headship of Christ.[169] It is this matter of *a modelled leadership* that is so exceptionally crucial that Satan himself has labored to undermine it throughout time, just as he did in the garden with the first family.

The principle of upholding *Solus Christus* and *Sola Scriptura* in both home and church is simple enough in theory, but the practice of it is much more challenging. Any ministry model which undermines the role of the husband/father by offering surrogate methods of family discipleship must be rejected. Though it may be tempting for some to think that men can and should delegate their responsibilities to others, all such thinking must be abandoned and replaced with the scriptural mandate of Ephesians 6:4. Any man, whether in leadership or not, who supposes that he can shirk his calling in the home should consider the danger of such hypocrisy. In his book, *Pilgrim's Progress,* Bunyan introduces his readers to a character named Talkative. As the name suggests, Talkative was a man who could talk all day about spirituality and Christian duty, but his conduct seen in public did not match what he was in private:

> "He [Talkative] talketh of prayer, of repentance, of faith, and of the new birth; but he knows but only to talk of them. I have been in his family, and have observed him both at home and abroad; and I know what I say of him is the truth. His house is as empty of religion as the white of an egg is of savor. There is there neither prayer, nor sign of repentance for sin; yea, the brute, in his kind, serves God far better than he. He is the very stain, reproach, and shame of religion to all that know him, Rom. 2:24, 25; it can hardly have a good word in all that end of the town where he dwells, through him. Thus say the common people that

---

[169] 1 Corinthians 11:3: But I want you to understand that Christ is the head of every man, and the man is the head of a woman, and God is the head of Christ.

know him, 'A saint abroad, and a devil at home.' His poor family finds it so; he is such a churl, such a railer at, and so unreasonable with his servants, that they neither know how to do for or speak to him. Men that have any dealings with him say, It is better to deal with a Turk than with him, for fairer dealings they shall have at their hands. This Talkative (if it be possible) will go beyond them, defraud, beguile, and overreach them. Besides, he brings up his sons to follow his steps; and if he finds in any of them a foolish timorousness, (for so he calls the first appearance of a tender conscience,) he calls them fools and blockheads, and by no means will employ them in much, or speak to their commendation before others. For my part, I am of opinion that he has, by his wicked life, caused many to stumble and fall; and will be, if God prevents not, the ruin of many more."[170]

Satan always seeks to direct men to be *saints abroad and devils as home.* Frankly speaking, this is easy enough even without his sordid help. Believers must be careful to guard against all incipient forms of compromise that would denigrate Christ's authority in the home and in the church. As well, the church must remember that the responsibilities of the overseer are quite grave. He is to be one who *is continually becoming an example to the flock,* understanding that his character qualities should direct others to the priority of exalting Christ and His authority, not himself or anything/anyone else. The pathway to corruption is always just a step away, and therefore we must walk circumspectly knowing that the days are evil.[171]

No man is above or beyond the warnings of Scripture, and the most pious among us must remember that he will always need to grow and improve in this life, *for let him who thinks he stands take heed, lest he fall.* It is for this reason that I still have that little paperback book that I harvested from the discount bin of my

---

[170] Bunyan, *The Pilgrim's Progress.*
[171] Ephesians 5:15-16.

favorite bookstore. It stands in my library as a pillar of warning to my own frail soul.

MY BANNER IS CHRIST

~ CHAPTER VIII ~

SOLUS CHRISTUS

IN THE LAND

OF BEULAH

It is crucial for the church to magnify Christ and His word against all opposition. Satan's constant attempt to distract and undermine God's people will not end until our Lord and Savior returns in judgment. As well, fathers and their families must contend earnestly for the faith, lest the Devil's corruptions creep in unnoticed.[172] Those fathers who wish to remain complacent and indifferent in this spiritual warfare endanger themselves and those under their charge. Whether in the home or in the church, human indifference to error and evil is a grave and dangerous sin. Not only is this true regarding the training of children, but it is true for all who name the name of Christ. Thus, all brethren must be well rooted and grounded in God's word lest Satan's weeds take root in our lives. Not only should we look with discernment at the world's influences, but we must also be careful regarding all that comes to us in the name of godly wisdom, remembering that Satan even appears as an angel of light. An undiscerning church is a dangerous place to be, especially in view of the countless voices promoted within modern media. As stated before, my point is not to vilify everything that modern media has to supply, but I am calling for the church to exercise better discernment amidst the current culture of celebritism. What we are all called to observe is the simplicity and purity of devotion to Christ, not men. This must be our priority in life as individuals, and it must be our priority for the local church. We have already consulted 1 Peter 5:1-4 in relation to the overseer's transparent ministry before the church, but we should further consider his conclusion of that section:

1 Peter 5:4: And when the Chief Shepherd appears, you will receive the unfading crown of glory.

Peter's reference to the Savior as the *Chief* Shepherd should remind every pastor that the church consists of Christ's sheep for whom He died (John 10:11-18); that the church is His possession by His shed blood (Acts 20:28); and that the church is His chosen bride for whom He will someday return (John 3:29-30, Ephesians 1-5, Revelation 19:7-10). Thus, the duty of the pastor is to serve as a mere doorkeeper whose task it is to look for the Good Shepherd, open the door of the sheepfold *to Him* while removing any encumbrance that would prevent the sheep from following Christ (John 10:1-5). Ultimately, 1 Peter 5:4 issues the important reminder that elders are merely *under-shepherds* who serve at the behest of the *Chief Shepherd, Jesus Christ.* Thus, their ministry does not center on themselves, but centers on Christ above all. Pastoral ministry, at its best, is that which magnifies and heralds the only Shepherd who is perfect and without sin. As already noted, 1 Peter 5:3 reminds us that pastors are not infallible and fixed statues set before the people, instead, they are fallible men whose lives are progressively growing and maturing before a watching church: *nor yet as lording it over those allotted to your charge, but proving to be [literally - becoming] examples to the flock.* When sheep can *directly see* their overseers submitting to the Chief Shepherd's authority, while growing in wisdom and devotion to God, they are able to model such examples of heralding *Solus Christus* and *Sola Scriptura* in their own lives. It is in this very context that Christ's sheep are called upon to *obey their leaders and submit to them* in view of their *life and doctrine*[173] *as qualified under-shepherds of the Chief Shepherd (1 Peter 5:4):*

Hebrews 13:17: Obey your leaders, and submit to them; for they keep watch over your souls, as those who will give an account. Let them do this with joy and not with grief, for this would be unprofitable for you.

---

[173] 1 Timothy 4:16.

This important relationship between Christ's sheep and their overseers certainly does not preclude the aid and assistance of all outside teachers and counsellors; yet, it does remind us of the importance of *the priority of the local church and its local leaders.* Taken together, 1 Peter 5:1-4 and Hebrews 13:17 remind us that deference must be given to the overseers of the local church, beneath the ultimate authority of Holy Writ, when considering scriptural instruction, doctrinal questions, personal counselling, or even theological disputes. As well, this principle should also remind us that the pastor, author, or conference speaker *of another church* is, in fact, *the pastor, author, or conference speaker of another church.* However prominent such an individual may be, he is not *your pastor, nor are you under his watch-care.* As simple of an observation this may be, it seems to be one that has fallen on hard times. In the modern era it is quite easy for individuals to be so caught up in the public ministry of a popular teacher that they no longer seek the counsel and shepherding care of their local church and church leaders. Additionally, the contemporary trend of women preachers has led countless women to bypass the shepherding ministry of their own husbands[174] and pastors for the female-celebrities of their choosing. This dangerous habit continues to be amplified in our new world of modern media.

Another crucial ministry that shepherds have within the ether of modern media consists of helping Christ's sheep discern the difference between core and clear doctrines of Scripture versus fruitless and foolish controversies (2 Timothy 2:14, 23, Titus 3:9, 1 Timothy 6:4). Anyone who has bothered to peruse the internet or a local bookstore can easily find resources which magnify marginal or even false teachings. The internet itself has proven to be a

---

[174] 1 Corinthians 14:34-35.

breeding ground for questionable teachings, conspiracy theories, or even rank gossip, all of which is poison to Christ's body. It is in this sense that Shepherds must endeavor to help Christ's sheep discern the differences between sound doctrine[175] and conspiratorial nonsense:[176]

> Titus 3:9: But shun foolish controversies and genealogies and strife and disputes about the Law; for they are unprofitable and worthless.

According to Paul, some disputes are so foolish and worthless that they must be shunned. On the other hand, as we have already seen with Paul's confrontations at Galatia, there are some doctrinal disputes that are quite serious and therefore must not be ignored at all. In view of this, we should consider the important subject of discernment, especially as it relates to matters that are worthy of debate. In particular, we will examine the difference between what many call *primary and secondary doctrines*, or *essentials and non-essentials*. This subject brings to mind that common expression historically attributed to Augustine:

> "In essentials, unity; in non-essentials, liberty; and in all things, charity."

It should be self-evident that brethren who share the *essential* convictions that are foundational to the Gospel can also have charitable disagreements over *non-essentials*, or *secondary doctrines*. Of course, this is much more difficult to apply in real life, but it does supply an important principle for us to consider. Yet, we still must evaluate the distinction between primary (essential) doctrines versus secondary (non-essential) doctrines. To do this, consider Paul's emphasis on the centrality of the Gospel in this passage:

---

[175] Titus 2:1.

[176] 2 Timothy 2:14, 23, Titus 3:9, 1 Timothy 6:4.

1 Corinthians 15:1–4: 1 NOW I make known to you, brethren, the gospel which I preached to you, which also you received, in which also you stand, 2 by which also you are saved, if you hold fast the word which I preached to you, unless you believed in vain. 3 For I delivered to you as of first importance what I also received, that Christ died for our sins according to the Scriptures, 4 and that He was buried, and that He was raised on the third day according to the Scriptures...

Paul refers to the central work of Christ as being a message *of first importance.* The simple language that he employs, along with the broader context of the chapter, points to the notion of *the primacy of the Gospel.* In other words, the Gospel is so central to the Christian faith that without it, there is no Christianity, as Paul attests later in the same chapter:

1 Corinthians 15:12–19: 12 Now if Christ is preached, that He has been raised from the dead, how do some among you say that there is no resurrection of the dead? 13 But if there is no resurrection of the dead, not even Christ has been raised; 14 and if Christ has not been raised, then our preaching is vain, your faith also is vain. 15 Moreover we are even found to be false witnesses of God, because we witnessed against God that He raised Christ, whom He did not raise, if in fact the dead are not raised. 16 For if the dead are not raised, not even Christ has been raised; 17 and if Christ has not been raised, your faith is worthless; you are still in your sins. 18 Then those also who have fallen asleep in Christ have perished. 19 If we have hoped in Christ in this life only, we are of all men most to be pitied.

Thus, the fact of Christ's death, burial, resurrection, and future advent[177] are all primary or essential truths. Without these core truths, there is no Gospel. Yet, Paul's teaching should not fall prey to a minimalistic form of thinking which neglects other doctrines

---

[177] Acts 17:30-31.

which uphold the Gospel. Thus, Paul's mention of Christ, the cross, sin, and the final resurrection implicitly points to a larger array of scriptural truths regarding Theology Proper (the nature and work of the Triune God), Christology (the doctrine of Christ), Harmartiology (the doctrine of mankind's sin), Soteriology (the doctrine of salvation), and the *core doctrine* of Eschatology (the doctrine of God's final judgment and redemption of mankind). My use of the expression *core doctrine of Eschatology* points to the Gospel truth of Christ's coming judgment of mankind and redemption of His people: a truth which all Christians believe. Paul made it clear that this truth was indelibly linked to the Gospel when he preached in the city of Athens:

> Acts 17:30–31: 30 "Therefore having overlooked the times of ignorance, God is now declaring to men that all everywhere should repent, 31 because He has fixed a day in which He will judge the world in righteousness through a Man whom He has appointed, having furnished proof to all men by raising Him from the dead."

The fact that Christ will return to judge mankind and establish His eternal kingdom is an unquestioned hope of all Christians, despite the church's historic variations of eschatological thinking. Throughout history the church has held to a variety of views regarding the details of Christ's return and reign, coming in the form of Amillennialism, Postmillennialism, Historic Premillennialism, and Dispensational Premillennialism. Such variance does not nullify the primary (essential) truth of Christ's coming return, after all, Amillennialists, Postmillennialists, Historic Premillennialists and Dispensational Premillennialists unequivocally stand fast on the unimpeachable truth of the Gospel: *that Christ laid down His life for His bride – the church, He rose again on the third day, and is coming again to judge the living and the dead and establish His eternal kingdom.* Thus, genuine believers throughout history have all shared the hope of the Chief Shepherd's Second Advent (an essential or primary doctrine), but they have varied on the question of the timing and administration of His return (a non-essential or secondary doctrine). Thus, may it never be said that Christian piety and orthodoxy is the sole purview of just one eschatological viewpoint within the realm of genuine Christian faith. This consideration is important because, whenever secondary doctrines are elevated to the station of primary doctrines, much division and confusion is produced. Therefore, Christ's under-shepherds have an important leadership responsibility before a watching flock: to herald the Gospel truth that *the Chief Shepherd is risen and is returning again.* The church can and should have its collegial debates about the particulars of eschatology, provided that she remembers that *this is a collegial discussion among brethren.*

For the church to fail at this matter of distinguishing primary and secondary doctrines poses a great danger. Those who treat everything in Scripture as having equal primacy with the Gospel tend to lack charity when dealing with others over *non-essentials.* Alternately, classic liberalism treats all doctrine as *secondary,* thus relegating the Bible into the trash heap of irrelevance.[178] All such extreme approaches to the Scriptures must be avoided. Where the Scriptures are clear and certain, the believer must be also. When it comes to matters of mystery[179] or issues that are debatable among those who embrace the Gospel, liberty and charity should prevail. Such an approach to the word should be promoted and upheld within the ministry of the church so that believers can pursue the

---

[178] "My conclusion was plain... I did not have to believe anything simply because it was in the Bible. The old basis of authority was gone. Truth was an open field to be explained. Nothing could be settled by a text." Harry Emerson Fosdick, The Living of These Days (New York: Harper & Brothers), 52.

[179] Deuteronomy 29:29.

simplicity and purity of devotion to Christ. As stated before, the principle is simple enough but what is more complex is the application of it, especially within the world of modern media.

Over the years I have come to the opinion that few popular teachers truly understand the *extent* of divisiveness that they can easily generate when they act imprudently over issues of doctrine, especially when such issues that are not central to the Gospel. In situations like these, it is not a question of heresy versus orthodoxy; instead, it becomes a concern over necessary debates versus doubtful disputations. All believers must guard against this matter of provoking useless controversies, especially in light of our need to labor *for the unity of the faith in the fear of Christ.* Should we err on a point of doctrine, or overemphasize a matter which results in unnecessary conflict, then we need to take responsibility for such matters for our own sakes and for the sake of those whom we influence – *from the pulpit to the pew.* When this happens in the context of the local church, the offending brother can correct his excesses, and those who were thus affected can immediately experience the benefits of the reversal. However, when such indiscretions are committed by prominent individuals, the process of correcting doctrinal excess or error becomes much more complex, especially when dealing with the recipients of such excess or error. My own experiences with this are too numerous to itemize, but the memory of being openly confronted by others over points of doctrine that bordered on heresy (as presented in the study notes in their Bible) comes to mind. When doctrinal excess or error is spread as far and wide as the publishing industry or internet can go, the process of correction becomes much more complicated because of sheer volume. In view of this, I would suggest that a man's personal responsibility as a teacher increases in proportion to the depth and breadth of his pedagogic influence.

I was reminded of all of this some time ago when a man came to visit our church for Sunday morning services. This man endured 1½ hours of driving in order to fellowship with us, hear God's word, and ask me a question that was burning in his conscience. Sensing his desire to speak at length about what was burdening him, I invited him over to our home for lunch following the services. We had a wonderful time of fellowship together. We spoke for some time before he eventually asked me his core question. His query brought little surprise to me in light of past experience. Some of the things that he had already said and even the study Bible that he held in hand made his question rather understandable. His question was simple enough: he wanted to know if he should leave his church since his pastor wasn't a dispensational premillennialist. The basis for his query came from his repeated exposure to an audio tape of John MacArthur issuing a millennial manifesto, where he said: *"Every self-respecting Calvinist is a premillennialist."* This gentleman repeated this manifesto thrice, saying "it keeps going on in my mind." It was quite clear that this doctrinal meditation of his only increased his sense of burden and concern. Before addressing my thoughts about such "self-respecting Calvinism," I asked this man questions about his present church. For all I knew, there could be other issues that would actually warrant significant concerns. I asked about his church's core doctrine (very sound); the body dynamic and health of the flock (loving and lively); the leadership – their doctrine and example of life (above reproach); and inquired about their focus on the Gospel and outreach to the lost (excellent). I am only summarizing the exchange here, but by the time he was finished describing his flock, I nearly wept in the man's presence. Though I had been aware of this controversy produced by MacArthur's manifesto, I was still struck by the practical effects that it continued to have in the lives of real people within real churches. Here was a man who was prepared to leave a loving flock over this matter. Wanting to be careful and measured in my response to him, I began discussing the extent of the controversy in its modern form (i.e., historic Pre-millennialism vs. Dispensational Pre-millennialism); the overall debate in view of church history; the relevance and purpose of prophecy in the life of a Christian; and the importance of the primacy of the Gospel in everything. I then told him "...with all due respect, no 'self-respecting Calvinist' would make eschatology such a divisive issue." I don't think that this gentleman expected to hear this from an alumnus of The Master's Seminary, but he listened carefully and attentively anyway. The strength of this man's devotion to MacArthur and his millennial manifesto was quite stunning at first, yet our conversation over the Scriptures eventually gave him a measure of pause. My simple prayer for this man was that he would pray and think through this matter very carefully. I encouraged him to go back to his elders and do what he had not yet done: speak openly with them about his concerns with his Bible in hand. As well, I reminded him that the thought of leaving one's church body is quite serious and, based upon what he had shared with me, I saw no reason for him to leave, *period.*

When I first heard MacArthur employ this manifesto, I was struck by his dogma and insistence. I certainly celebrate his freedom to believe what he does, but when one considers what is conveyed in his assertion, it is all quite striking. MacArthur's version of Dispensational Pre-Millennialism formulates the centerpiece of what he calls self-respecting Calvinism. The implications of his charge are as follows: anyone who does not hold to such Pre-Millennialism *is not a self-respecting Calvinist.* Moreover, the strength of his charge is only reinforced by the following:

"Let's leave Amillennialism for the Arminians. It's perfect. It's ideal. It's a no-brainer. God elects nobody and preserves nobody. Perfect.

Arminians make great Amillennialists....We can leave Amillennialism to the process theologians or the openness people who think God is becoming what He will be; and He's getting better because as every day goes by, He gets more information; and as He gets more information, He's figuring out whether or not, in fact, He can keep some of the promises He made without having to adjust all of them based upon a lack of information when He originally made them. Let's leave Amillennialism to the Charismatics and the semi-Pelagians and other sorts who go in and out of salvation willy-nilly; it makes sense for their theology."[180]

Postmillennialism isn't given any better treatment when he says:

"...Postmillennialism... is 'optimistic Amillennialism'...the two positions are basically the same."[181]

If anyone wishes to search out the oddities and heresies associated with *any system of eschatology*, they are certainly welcome to do so, but is this helpful? For example, Harold Camping (a dispensational premillennialist) was a self-declared prophet who is well known for his failed prediction of the return of Christ on May 21st 2011, despite the clear teachings of Scripture.[182] Thus, comparing MacArthur to a false teacher like Camping is a fool's errand and takes us no-where. Samuel Waldron rightly refutes such guilt by association argumentation in his book, *MacArthur's Millennial Manifesto – A Friendly Response*:

"One of my correspondents pointed out that the Church was dominantly Roman Catholic for this millennium and that Roman Catholicism is Amillennial. This is supposed to be an argument against

---

[180] John MacArthur, Why Every Self-Respecting Calvinist is a Premillennialist, Shepherds' Conference 2007, First Message.
[181] Ibid.
[182] Acts 1:7.

Amillennialism. Not only does this forget that Luther and Calvin remained Amillennial when leaving Rome, it also forgets that this kind of argument is a two-edged sword. yes, we have most Roman Catholics on our side, but the Premillenialist has the Jehovah's Witnesses, Seventh Day Adventists, and the Church of Jesus Christ of Latter-Day Saints as fellow Premillennialists. The point is that this kind of argumentation proves nothing. It is guilt by association." [183]

In the above text, Waldron is responding to those who have argued that Amillennialism's historic association with Roman Catholicism makes it entirely suspect. Yet, is it really fair to associate the whole of Amillennialism with the likes of Roman Catholicism, just as MacArthur does with process or openness theologians? Arguments of guilt-by-association can be very startling, and may *seem* to justify a host of accusations, but such arguments don't advance any reasonable or meaningful debate. It is not terribly surprising that those who hear such statements are quickly led to the fearful belief that Amillennialism directly corresponds to various forms of *rank heresy*. Shocking claims like these make it perfectly understandable that our anxious visitor came to me with such a manifesto resonating in his mind, wondering if he should leave his church immediately. It is understandable, but it is all quite sad and disturbing.

In a world where the Gospel, the primacy of Christ, the authority of Scripture, and the institution of marriage are all under violent attack, it is quite clear that Christ's body has far more central concerns that should occupy her time and attention. Collegial debates over secondary doctrines related to eschatology should be pursued, but they should not impede the front line of battle that believers face in a hostile world. All believers should take heed

---

[183] Samuel E. Waldron, MacArthur's Millennial Manifesto – A Friendly Response (KY, Owensboro: Reformed Baptist Academic Press), p. 17.

unto themselves regarding their own doctrinal priorities and avoid any form of thinking which majors on the minors of life. MacArthur's choice to stress dispensational premillennialism in this manner is somewhat ironic, especially when one considers the short history of dispensational premillennialism. From the early 20th century to the present day, churches that have had an inordinate emphasis on dispensational premillennialism have typically demonstrated a weakness on several core doctrines centered on the Gospel. My aforementioned conflict, while serving in the Midwest, exemplifies the dangers of majoring on non-essential contests. In that situation, the church's historic focus on premillennial eschatology, as well as dispensationalism as a system of doctrine, distracted it from the core Scriptural truths regarding theology proper and the Gospel itself. Whenever millenarianism becomes the centerpiece of our thinking and concern, we can be sure that we have drifted from the true centerpiece of all prophecy: Jesus Christ Himself. Waldron offers a helpful word of caution in response to MacArthur's quandary regarding Amillennialism's historic association with Reformed teaching:

"What has MacArthur calmly admitted in these statements? He has admitted that the major historical defenders of his understanding of sovereign grace and election have consistently rejected his eschatology. MacArthur thinks that Calvinistic views of election ought to lead-in fact, must logically and clearly lead-to Premillennial views of eschatology. Yet, and in stunning contrast, Church history shows just the opposite connection. The major proponents of sovereign election have been also the major advocates of Amillennialism. Augustine (an Amillennialist) almost single-handedly opposed the insidious and centuries-long drift of the early church into Pelagianism."[184]

---

[184] Ibid.

Waldron's statement is not supplied in order to exalt Amillennialism over Premillennialism, but to point out the difference between primary and secondary doctrines. The flagrant notion of associating Amillennialism with Semi-Pelagianism and the heresy of Open Theism is almost unworthy of a serious response. Augustine's legacy and contribution to the church, through his strenuous refutations of Pelagianism, is a powerful testament to the importance of heralding primary doctrines over secondary ones. This stands as another pillar of warning for those who would inadvertently diminish the priority of the Gospel for the sake of intermural debates over non-essentials. Whenever a particular view of eschatology is heralded at the level of the Gospel itself, or higher, the seeds of error will grow and thrive in time. Ironically, it was this very theological culture that MacArthur confronted with the historic doctrines of grace during the 90's. His helpful book, *The Gospel According to Jesus,* created a firestorm of controversy among many Dispensationalists in view of its affirmation of God's sovereign grace in salvation. For a man who had to face the errors of a culture which exalted Dispensationalism and Premillennialism above its theological place, one must wonder why he would seek such a contest as this in the present day. Only time will tell what impact all this will have on those who are influenced by MacArthur's teachings. By mentioning these concerns, the point is not to dismiss the full spectrum of MacArthur and his preaching of the Gospel. One point of critical analysis is not equivalent a complete censure of a man and his ministry. Though this point may be self-evident to most, it has become necessary to underscore in our contemporary world of celebritism. As we have repeatedly noted, no man is exempt from a biblical critique for the sake of the Gospel. Though I do not agree entirely with Waldron's eschatology, I do appreciate his careful and irenic spirit regarding the conflict:

"...there is at least one thing I love more than our dear brother (John MacArthur). It is truth. MacArthur set forth nothing less than a Dispensational and Premillennial manifesto...his message embodies significant misrepresentations of Amillennialism and vastly confuses the true nature of the debate between Dispensational Premillennialism and Amillennialism."[185] "There are some whom MacArthur has angered by his manifesto. I do feel misrepresented and misunderstood by a badly misinformed brother. I am not aware, however, of being angry. In fact, this brings me to my fundamental reason for responding which is simply to set the record straight. No one who thinks he understands the Scriptures on an important point can bear to see others misrepresent views he believes are thoroughly biblical... How then can we endure seeing our views drastically misrepresented? We cannot and allegiance to the truth demands that we respond."[186]

Waldron's simple and gracious appeal for the pursuit of truth is to be commended. Moreover, since MacArthur has placed such a premium on this subject, it would be helpful if he issued a public response to Waldron in the same pursuit of truth.[187] A collegial dialogue between these men would help others by demonstrating the importance of open dialogue amidst theological controversy. In the end, we should remember that, before Christ, the church, and a watching world, all brethren must carefully consider the manner in which intermural contests are pursued, especially when they involve interpretive questions that are not central to the Gospel. Love for Christ should compel us to such a consideration. As those who proclaim the power of God's sovereign grace to save and sanctify sinners, we ought to be gracious in our dealings with others. As well, we should spend more of our energy emphasizing the unifying truth concerning the Lord's second coming. Of the

---

[185] Ibid, 2.

[186] Ibid, 4.

[187] According to my knowledge, no such response has been issued by MacArthur as of the writing of this manuscript.

full spectrum of eschatological views representing the true church, one common thread connects them all – *an anxious longing for the Lord Jesus Christ:*

> Philippians 3:20: For our citizenship is in heaven, from which also we *eagerly wait for a Savior, the Lord Jesus Christ*;

> Jude 21: keep yourselves in the love of God, *waiting anxiously for the mercy of our Lord Jesus Christ to eternal life.*

Here is a *primary doctrine* that ought to be pressed and emphasized: the true child of God has an *eager and anxious longing* for Christ and His return (1 Corinthians 1:7, Titus 2:13, Hebrews 9:28, 2 Peter 3:12, Jude 21, Philippians 3:20). Whatever persuasion of eschatology one may have, such an anxious longing for Christ will be found in the bosom of all those who love Christ truly. Bunyan's reflection on this central truth in, *The Pilgrim's Progress*, is quite strong. Just before Christian and Hopeful would enter Heaven (the Celestial City), they came to a land called *Beulah (Marriage:* Isaiah 62:4–12[188]). It is here that their longing for Christ intensified in view of the coming marriage of the Lamb and His chosen bride:

> "Now, as they walked in this land, they had more rejoicing than in parts more remote from the kingdom to which they were bound; and drawing near to the city, they had yet a more perfect view thereof: It was builded of pearls and precious stones, also the streets thereof were paved with gold; so that, by reason of the natural glory of the city, and

---

[188] Isaiah 62:4–5: 4 It will no longer be said to you, "Forsaken," Nor to your land will it any longer be said, "Desolate"; But you will be called, "My delight is in her," And your land, "Married"; For the LORD delights in you, And to Him your land will be married.5 For as a young man marries a virgin, So your sons will marry you; And as the bridegroom rejoices over the bride, So your God will rejoice over you.

the reflection of the sunbeams upon it, Christian with desire fell sick; Hopeful also had a fit or two of the same disease: wherefore here they lay by it a while, crying out because of their pangs, 'If you see my Beloved, tell him that I am sick of love.'"

The imagery of a bride and bridegroom longing anxiously to be together in holy matrimony is the very scriptural picture that Bunyan illustrates for us from Isaiah 62:4-12 and other texts. Clearly, men of varying eschatological persuasions can have their differences about the finer details of Christ's return, *but all brethren should labor most intensely so as to promote a deeper longing for the One who is the centerpiece of all eschatological doctrine.* Should we fail at this primary emphasis of doctrine, then we fall short of the Lord's purpose for prophetic revelation: *Blessed is he who reads and those who hear the words of the prophecy, and heed the things which are written in it; for the time is near (Revelation 1:3).*

May Christ *alone* be the centerpiece of all our eschatological meditations, and may our longing for that eternal union burn so strongly within us, each and every passing day, that its intensity increases to the end. This is the hope and longing of all who believe in the Savior, and it is the hope and calling of the Gospel itself: that men need not perish in their sin, but through faith in Christ have everlasting life in the risen Savior, *forevermore.*

MY
BANNER
IS
CHRIST

~ CHAPTER IX ~

NOT ALL

ARE

TEACHERS

The world of Christian media is a bit of a two-edged sword. Through it many Bible teachers have helped the cause of the Gospel in the lives of many men and women. It is *this side* of the sword that cuts well – *for the glory of God*. Then there is the other side of this sword – the one which tends to spill more blood than supply corrective surgery. In this latter side of the blade we find the unhelpful and sometimes destructive influences of popular preachers/teachers whose misplaced dogmas and verbal mishaps find their way into the local church through various ways and means. The pastor of a local church may wish to ignore the presence of this bad side of the blade – but he hasn't the luxury to do so, especially if some of his congregants are the devoted disciples of such Bible teachers. With very little effort, churches can be caught up in controversies which have little basis or merit whatsoever. It is for this reason that pastors and congregants need to guard against any strife or division which undermines the priority of heralding Christ and His word.

Within the first few months of my experience as a pastor I became aware of a man who, for the sake of this section, will be referred to as Joe. When Joe first came to my office I did not readily recognize him as a member of our church for the simple reason that he rarely attended services, and up to that point I couldn't recall having met him any time prior. Joe visited me because he wanted to serve in a ministry where he would teach the Bible and serve the elderly, and all that was required was a signature from the pastor of his church. Uncertain about how I should respond, I received his application and kindly let him know that I would get back with him, seeing that the elders would be meeting soon. Joe was fine with this, and he went on his way. When I met with the elders, I informed them of Joe's request, but curiously inquired about who this gentleman was since I had no prior knowledge of him. Their comments were just as brief as was their counsel to me: they simply advised me to sign the form and consider myself done with the matter. Feeling somewhat uneasy about their advice, I then shifted the discussion a bit by asking them if they would be willing sign the form. Stunningly, they insisted that they wouldn't, *down to the last man.* As one of my earliest experiences in the ministry, this seemingly small event proved to be a massive and important lesson for me as a young pastor. Incredulous to their inconsistent responses, I then asked them to explain and justify why they were willing to advise me to do something that they themselves wouldn't. More particularly, I focused my queries on who Joe was and why they were so adamant about not signing his form. For the next several minutes, I listened to tale after tale about the problems and indiscretions of Joe. How he rarely attended the flock; had stirred some conflicts in the community; acted in a divisive manner with others when he did attend church; and failed to be responsive to the elder board. It was at this point that my conversation shifted from Joe to the elders themselves. I had no choice but to address two main concerns: first, I pointed out the leadership's failure to address Joe's longstanding problems in the context of loving church discipline and, second, I expressed concern over the fact that they were willing to have me sign a form, in ignorance to these problems, *in order to placate a man with several issues whom they considered to be quite unqualified for the task.* Upon reviewing several relevant Scriptures on the subject (Matt. 18:15-18, Titus 3:10) I proposed that we speak with Joe, explaining our reasons for not approving the form, while using this as an opportunity to work with a man whose problems had been ignored for so long. This would include admission and confession of the leadership's failure to address such concerns from the beginning. Joe's issues and problems were not only problematic regarding his desire to serve in a teaching and serving ministry, but they were fundamental enough to constitute a word of correction, counsel, and potentially, church discipline. Sadly, Joe wasn't willing to listen to our appeals and admissions. I didn't sign the form, and he was angry at all of us, especially me. It became apparent that Joe's unpleasant response was exactly what the elders feared and wanted to avoid. What transpired in the days and months following was quite remarkable. Joe began a lengthy campaign of letter writing, phone calls, and visits to my office. In this campaign of his, he endeavored to demonstrate just how qualified he was to serve in the ministry for which he applied. Over and over again, he recounted to me the multiple, well known mentors that he had in his life, the various forms of Bible training he had received, along with the countless seminars and conferences he had attended. On the few occasions that I met with him, Joe seemed to carry with him the ensigns of his credentials through the study Bible he used and some of the conference t-shirts and hats that he wore. In a sense, Joe carried many of his own heraldic banners – banners which, in his own thinking, identified his credibility as a mature Christian. All of the men that he named were *celebrated men* whose books, sermons, and radio programs were available to Joe, but none of them knew or shepherded Joe in any personal sense. To Joe, the concept of mentoring and discipleship was a very remote and isolated one where face to face accountability was non-existent. In the end, Joe's campaign to demonstrate his qualifications only revealed that he was a veritable graduate of *Celebrity Theological Seminary* and his "church" was nothing more than a loose collection of individuals whom he met over the years, one conference after another. With hindsight, I now look upon the events surrounding Joe as one grand lesson on the dangers of departing from *Solus Christus* and *Sola Scriputra*. For example, had the elders heralded Christ and His will above Joe and his demands, they would have approached him in love long ago. It is always a temptation for leaders to ignore issues in order to avoid painful controversy, but love for Christ leads us to a better pathway. Moreover, when church leaders fear men more than the Lord, they enter into dangerous areas of compromise. Concerning Joe, had he heralded Christ above his celebrity heroes, conferences, love for autonomy, and self-centered desires, he wouldn't be living his life as a theological lone-ranger, drifting from one place to another. Overall, the controversy with Joe was relatively mild compared to many other contests I have had to face over the years. Yet, one of the most painful realities about Joe's story is that there are many more like him, and not all are lone rangers. In larger church contexts where personal accountability is weak, men and women like Joe can carry on with their lives beneath the banner of this celebrity pastor or that popular conference speaker with little notice. For many such people, their local church is of inferior rank to their next parachurch experience, whatever that may be. Throughout the years, I have encountered a great number of individuals who are more committed to a popular personality who is highly acclaimed, in popular demand, and well published in the world of Christian media, than they are to a local flock. When such individuals are more inclined to quote such men as these than they are to quote scripture, it signifies a deep problem. Pastors who dare not contradict such evangelical celebrities, even when they know they should, are no better than the sycophants who follow them. Our fear of offending men should never eclipse our dread of offending God, as Flavel rightly asserts:

"Be more afraid of grieving God, or wounding conscience, than of displeasing or losing all the friends you have in the world besides; look upon every adventure upon sin to escape danger to be the same thing as if you should sink the ship to avoid one that you take to be a pirate."[189]

---

[189] Flavel, <u>A Practical Treatise of Fear</u>, p 306.

In the modern era, uninvited teachers often enter into the church *via* the internet or the printed page, and their potential for damage is magnified by their sheer volume and availability of all such materials. With respect to the internet, teachers and their teachings can "go viral" with breathtaking speed and their influences can be felt within the church well before the leadership can be made aware of it. As I have already pointed out, I am not issuing a draconian repudiation of all available resources online or in print (such an argument would make this book an act of abject hypocrisy); instead, I am reminding the reader that not all that glitters is gold among the host of teachers in the present day. The *means* by which modern media is published is not my concern, nor even the volume of materials it produces; instead it is the question of *who* is offering instruction, *why* are their teachings so popular, *what* are they teaching, is their teaching sound, and do their lives reflect the standards of what they teach? Too often these important questions are brushed aside as secondary to the irrelevant queries of what is "trending" or "going viral" amidst the pantheon of popular religious teaching today. While I celebrate the open opportunities for producing and distributing doctrinal materials for the good of the church, I am still concerned when the church utilizes these materials with little to no discernment.

Perhaps the greatest innovation of the 15th century was Johannes Gutenberg's printing press. This, coupled with the teachers, writers, and translators of the Reformation helped to launch a rediscovery of the Scriptures along with many rich theological teachings. Without the distribution of various tracts and booklets to advance such a rediscovery of the Scriptures, it seems impossible to imagine that the Reformation could ever have taken place. When we move forward to the present era, we find much more than Gutenberg's printing press. Today, we find a world that is overflowing with published materials via printed media as well as the internet. This has led to an explosion of instructional writings, videos, and audio recordings which make the days of Gutenberg's press seem like the dark ages rather than a renaissance. That said, with the open access to such materials, and the ease with which they can be created, we also find that all such materials range from the good, the bad, and the ugly – even to that which is evil. The free and open nature of the internet has created a virtual world in which, it would seem, *all are teachers.* The only problem is, not all are teachers nor should all assume such a task:

> James 3:1:   Let not many of you become teachers, my brethren, knowing that as such we will incur a stricter judgment.

James' warning, though quite serious, is too often ignored. We find this in Paul's corrections of the church at Corinth. One of the great problems at Corinth was that they arrogantly assumed that they possessed all of the gifts of the Spirit, rather than realizing that *not all are Apostles, not all are prophets, and not all are teachers.*[190] In all of this self-presumption of theirs they became poor students of genuine authority. As a result, they allowed a variety of errors into their ranks which justified a series of corrective letters from Paul. I would suggest that the problems found at Corinth somewhat illustrate the problems of the modern church in the internet age, where many presume to be teachers. This produces several problems: *1. It promotes a spirit of arrogance and independence among those who are not called by God to serve His church as teachers; 2. It can undermine the importance and relevancy of the teaching ministry of the local church; 3. It can produce vast numbers of "disciples" who remain strangers to their online "mentor(s);" and 4. It can undermine the importance of the husband's/father's calling to lead his household as its head.* As we

---

[190] 1 Corinthians 12:29: All are not apostles, are they? All are not prophets, are they? All are not teachers, are they? All are not workers of miracles, are they?

have already noted, pastors and teachers are called not only to exemplary doctrine, but they are also called to live exemplary lives as well. When these two elements are separated, a dangerous disconnect is created just as in the case of Bunyan's character, Talkative: a man who was *a saint abroad but a devil at home*. Simply put, if a modern-day Talkative could have access to the great expanse of the internet, his "ministry" could lead to the ruin of many souls. Without sound discernment, Christ's bride can find herself beneath the influences of one or many teachers with whom she has no personal relationship, whereby it cannot be known if they are *a devil at home*. It is for this reason that the plethora of instructors found within the world of modern media can pose as much danger to the church as it can help, or worse. This is not to say that only pastors can write and instruct. The point of concern being raised is this: a genuine teaching ministry is not designed by God to be conducted autonomously; instead, it is to be carried out *and witnessed* in the context of the church.

> 1 Thessalonians 1:5: for our gospel did not come to you in word only, but also in power and in the Holy Spirit and with full conviction; just as you know what kind of men we proved to be among you for your sake.

Clearly, Paul was no Talkative. By God's grace, there was a strong relationship between what he preached and how he lived, and this ministry impacted the Thessalonians deeply. *This is why the ministry of the local church cannot be replaced with an electronic substitute.*

MY BANNER IS CHRIST

~ CONCLUSION ~

THE PALACE

THAT IS CALLED

BEAUTIFUL

Clearly, much of the content of this book has heralded the priority of reverencing Christ and His word *in the local church*. However, this emphasis on the local church must not be seen as an advocacy for isolationism or extreme separatism; instead, the point is to strengthen the bonds between pastors and those whom they shepherd under the supreme authority of Christ. Another emphasis in this work has been on the subject of human sin and our unfortunate propensity towards man-centered idolatry: *celebritism* and *the fear of man*. The point of such a meditation is not to be depressive or morose, but to issue the reminder that we all need God's continual grace and wisdom in order to shun all stumbling blocks which impede a simplicity and purity of devotion to Christ. Satan's roadblocks are many, but God's merciful provisions are infinite. In all of this, one thing is for certain: on this side of heaven, we are all imperfect people in need of growth each and every day. Perfection will come someday, when He returns for His bride, but until then we must pursue growth and sanctification as individuals and collectively as churches. I realize that it isn't new news for me to tell you that you are imperfect and that the church you attend is imperfect. Yet, I issue such a reminder in order to direct attention to some important, concluding thoughts. The question we must consider is this: *how do we respond to sin and imperfection, especially when we perceive that there are problems or deficiencies within one's local church?* Whenever such concerns arise, we must be careful to apply biblical wisdom to our thinking lest we find ourselves pressing for unhelpful changes in Christ's body. An individual who is fully convinced that their church is doomed without a particular church program or musical style should carefully consider whether or not they are stressing primary doctrines or personal preferences. Especially in our modern age, these matters must be given special care and attention.

In a market-driven, consumer-based society such as ours, it is not uncommon for churches to conduct themselves, or be treated as, shopping markets which advertise their wares to a broad array of consumers. Amidst a mentality as this, the personal desires of consumers (congregants) formulate the centerpiece of "worship," and all ministry-products provided by the church must please the customer, or be returned without question. When dissatisfied with such service, the consumer simply goes elsewhere to another business (church). Such a church-marketing mechanism as this yields a debauched system whereby individuals simply migrate from one church to another until they find maximal satisfaction based upon their felt needs. The criteria of such church-shopping often hinges on lesser issues such as denominational affiliations; associations with various conferences, Evangelical-celebrities, parachurch organizations; youth ministries; church programs; and perhaps the most common one of them all: contemporary music and "worship bands." While such a shopping list has become nearly canonical in the modern day, *one must wonder where any of this can be found in Scripture.* Of course, Holy Writ directs us to something remarkably different than such a shallow shopping list; it gives believers the call to a servitude that is centered on God and others:

> Philippians 2:3–5: 3 Do nothing from selfishness or empty conceit, but with humility of mind let each of you regard one another as more important than himself; 4 do not merely look out for your own personal interests, but also for the interests of others. 5 Have this attitude in yourselves which was also in Christ Jesus,

Such servitude has, as its centerpiece, a love for God and for others:

> Mark 12:28–31: 28 And one of the scribes came and heard them arguing, and recognizing that He had answered them well, asked Him,

"What commandment is the foremost of all?" 29 Jesus answered, "The foremost is, 'HEAR, O ISRAEL! THE LORD OUR GOD IS ONE LORD; 30 AND YOU SHALL LOVE THE LORD YOUR GOD WITH ALL YOUR HEART, AND WITH ALL YOUR SOUL, AND WITH ALL YOUR MIND, AND WITH ALL YOUR STRENGTH.' 31 "The second is this, 'YOU SHALL LOVE YOUR NEIGHBOR AS YOURSELF.' There is no other commandment greater than these."

The above two texts offer a mere summary of the wealth of NT Scriptures dealing with the believer's calling to love and serve God and man. Such texts remind us that those who have been born from above no longer live on the basis of hedonistic selfishness; instead, their love for God leads them to love others, even their enemies.[191] Churches that are comprised of such selfless servants are sure to lack the consumer-based shopping lists of the modern day. Instead, such individuals will herald the Scriptural criteria for what a church should and must be, and they will be like those brethren whose worship and servitude Luke highlights in the book of Acts:

Acts 2:41–47: 41 So then, those who had received his word were baptized; and there were added that day about three thousand souls. 42 And they were continually devoting themselves to the apostles' teaching and to fellowship, to the breaking of bread and to prayer. 43 And everyone kept feeling a sense of awe [*phobos* - fear]; and many wonders and signs were taking place through the apostles. 44 And all those who had believed were together, and had all things in common; 45 and they began selling their property and possessions, and were sharing them with all, as anyone might have need. 46 And day by day

---

[191] Matthew 5:43–45: 43 "You have heard that it was said, 'YOU SHALL LOVE YOUR NEIGHBOR, and hate your enemy.' 44 "But I say to you, love your enemies, and pray for those who persecute you 45 in order that you may be sons of your Father who is in heaven; for He causes His sun to rise on the evil and the good, and sends rain on the righteous and the unrighteous.

continuing with one mind in the temple, and breaking bread from house to house, they were taking their meals together with gladness [*agalliasei* – extreme joy] and sincerity of heart [*apheloteti* - humility, simplicity], 47 praising [*ainountes*] God, and having favor with all the people. And the Lord was adding to their number day by day those who were being saved.

In the introduction of this book, we briefly looked at the joyful reverence of these early believers, yet we should look further into their affections and actions because they offer helpful insights for every generation. Before the tares of corruption had entered into the church, as evidenced at Corinth, Colossae, Galatia, and Ephesus, we find a certain *simplicity and purity of devotion to Christ* in these 1st century believers. In describing these brethren, Luke tells us nothing about musical styles or church programs; instead, he reveals some specific attitudes which characterized their worship: *fear, extreme joy, and sincerity of heart.* How *unsurprising* it is that the Holy Spirit would yield such affections for Christ in light of the Psalmist's important command regarding genuine worship: "Worship the LORD with reverence, and rejoice with trembling." (Psalm 2:11). Along with this, Luke mentions that these early believers had a humility, or sincerity of heart (*apheloteti*), which clearly indicates that they were no longer the prisoners of their own pride and hedonistic selfishness, but with gladness of heart, they shared their possessions with those in need as servants of Christ. As for their fear and extreme joy, such affections are evident in their continual devotion (*proskarterountes*)[192] to Christ's authoritative instructions for the church: *And they were continually devoting themselves to the apostles' teaching and to fellowship, to the breaking of bread and to*

---

[192] Luke's use of the present active participle of *proskartereō* reveals the perpetual nature of their devotion to Christ's authority and prescribed activities of the church.

prayer (Acts 2:42). These beautiful signs of genuine life in the Jerusalem church are deeply encouraging, for they direct us to the path and trajectory which honors Christ. Clearly, the church at Jerusalem was the very antithesis of the church at Sardis which had a reputation for being alive, even though it was dead.

In the current day, we must wonder if modern Evangelicalism will move in a trajectory which leans towards the church at Jerusalem, or towards the church at Sardis. Only time will tell, but in the meantime we must take heed unto ourselves and guard against the irreverence and shallowness of heart which leads to the graveyard of Sardis. We are all imperfect members of our respective flocks, and we must take care to grow in Christ and thereby become better contributors to our respective assemblies. Should we be concerned about the station and direction of our churches, then we must be careful to measure our concerns by the standards of God's word and not by what the contemporary culture is doing. If our churches are growing in devotion to Christ and His word (*Solus Christus* and *Sola Scriptura*), as seen in the simplicity of worship at Jerusalem, then we should thank God for this and pray for His increase in such a direction. Beyond this, we must guard against the temptation and pressure to stir strife over lesser matters. Churches that are able to grow in such a simplicity and purity of devotion to Christ represent the same kind of church piety, fellowship, and mission described by Bunyan in *The Pilgrim's Progress*. Bunyan called such an ideal church *The Palace Beautiful* which represented a non-conformist fellowship that was free of the encumbrances of English rule. Barry Horner expands upon Bunyan's symbolism regarding *The Palace Beautiful:*

"Here is an exquisitely beautiful and extensive portrayal of a faithful biblical local church, a nonconformist assembly, an outpost of the

Celestial City (heaven), so necessary if sustained progress is to be maintained..." [193]

Horner expands upon Bunyan's understanding of the true church's interest in, and focus on, the need for its members to have saving faith in Christ:

"...careful distinction is made here between Bunyan's belief in a separated church gathered out of sinful society and the comprehensive Church of England establishment that was wedded to the state, with the monarch as its head. In other words, local church membership in a nonconformist fellowship required a testimony to regeneration and personal salvation, in contrast with the merely nominal association with the Church of England to which the populace in general were admitted through the formal administration of the outward ritual of baptism." [194]

The Gospel is a direct threat to man-centered religion because it points to and heralds the true Head and Lord of the church. It is for this reason that many pastors in this period were persecuted for their commitment to the authority of Christ and His word alone. As noted earlier, Bunyan was imprisoned for his unwillingness to cease from preaching the Gospel, but he wasn't the only victim of such a draconian treatment of nonconformist preachers:

"Upon the accession of Charles II to the throne after the Restoration of the monarchy in 1660, opposition by independent churches to legally mandated conformity led to Bunyan's immediate imprisonment as well

---

[193] Barry E. Horner, Pilgrim's Progress – Themes and Issues (MA: Auburn, Evangelical Press, 2003), 261.

[194] Horner, Pilgrim's Progress, 295.

as the ejection of about 1,760 Dissenting ministers from their pastorates." [195]

Thus, Bunyan's depiction of The Palace Beautiful in *The Pilgrim's Progress* offers important reminders regarding the true church's conflict and opposition in this world. As soon as Christian saw the palace he proceeded towards it, but was momentarily hindered by the sight of two lions on either side of the road. He then recalled meeting two men earlier, Mistrust and Timorous, who were traveling to the city of Zion until they saw the lions and ran away in fear. Christian, also fearful for his life, proceeded with great trepidation until the Porter of the palace (i.e., a doorkeeper – pastor: John 10:3) called upon him to press on firmly in faith:

> "But the Porter at the lodge, whose name is Watchful, perceiving that Christian made a halt, as if he would go back, cried unto him, saying, 'Is thy strength so small?' Mark 4:40. 'Fear not the lions, for they are chained, and are placed there for trial of faith where it is, and for discovery of those that have none: keep in the midst of the path, and no hurt shall come unto thee.'"

Bunyan helps us to see several important principles in this portion of his allegory. *First,* he shows us the great danger of fearing anything or anyone but God alone. Christian had become paralyzed with fear until the Porter exhorted him to cease from such fear and proceed on his journey. Only then was he able to make progress in the right direction. *Second,* once Christian came to the palace, he asked the Porter about whose house it was. The Porter's answer was this: "This house was built by the Lord of the hill, and he built it for the *relief* and *security* of pilgrims." Bunyan's use of the words *relief* and *security* remind us of what the church must supply for Christ's sheep. Genuine *relief* comes to the

---

[195] Ibid.

believer's heart through a trust in Christ and the heralding of His authoritative word; however, beneath the banner of faux religion, the people will become distressed and dispirited as sheep without a shepherd (Matthew 9:36). The church is also to be a place of spiritual *security* for Christ's sheep rather than a place of danger. We are reminded of Jude's prophetic rebukes of those wolves who had *crept in unnoticed* within the walls of the church, seeking to ravage the sheep. Shepherds who allow such carnage are not shepherds at all because the church must be a haven of safety. *Third,* Christian was greeted by Piety, Prudence, and Charity who reviewed and discussed his testimony of faith and his progress of life. In this lengthy portion of the narrative, Bunyan shows us just how important it is for the church to receive into its membership only those who have genuine faith in Christ. As already noted, to its own detriment, the Church of England required no such scrutiny. Yet, in The Palace Beautiful, those who had genuine faith were eagerly received and with great joy they feasted on their conversation about the Savior and His redeeming love:

> "Now the table was furnished with fat things, and with wine that was well refined; and all their talk at the table was about the Lord of the hill; as, namely, about what he had done, and wherefore he did what he did, and why he had builded that house; and by what they said, I perceived that he had been a great warrior, and had fought with and slain him that had the power of death, Heb. 2:14, 15; but not without great danger to himself, which made me love him the more."[196]

The richness of their godly dialogue was then followed by an important step for Christian, which depicts the goal and priority of every Christian within the church:

---

[196] Bunyan, *The Pilgrim's Progress.*

MY BANNER IS CHRIST

"The next day they took him, and had him into the armoury, where they showed him all manner of furniture which their Lord had provided for pilgrims, as sword, shield, helmet, breastplate, all-prayer, and shoes that would not wear out. And there was here enough of this to harness out as many men for the service of their Lord as there be stars in the heaven for multitude."[197]

It is in this crucial station (the armoury) that Christian was equipped with the full armour of God and thereby readied for the remainder of his journey to his heavenly home. As for the bounty of supplies found within the armoury, Bunyan reminds us that *there was enough of this to harness out as many men for the service of their Lord as there be stars in the heaven for multitude.* Within this small section of *The Pilgrim's Progress* we have a simple yet beautiful picture of what Christ's church is designed to do: to equip Christ's sheep amidst a world of great, Satanic hostility:

Ephesians 6:11–13: 11 Put on the full armour of God, that you may be able to stand firm against the schemes of the devil. 12 For our struggle is not against flesh and blood, but against the rulers, against the powers, against the world forces of this darkness, against the spiritual forces of wickedness in the heavenly places. 13 Therefore, take up the full armour of God, that you may be able to resist in the evil day, and having done everything, to stand firm.

Bunyan's allegory illustrates the profound truth of Scripture which teaches that all of the power and authority of this dark world is impotent against Christ and His church. The world forces of this darkness will rage on a daily basis, and it will issue its deceptions and temptations to the church without end. Should we see Satan's lions, we must remember that they are chained and restrained by

---

[197] Ibid.

our sovereign Lord who alone has the keys of death and Hades.[198] Our place of safety is in the pathway of *His truth* and the building of *His making,* rather than in this world which is passing away. May it be that our estimation of the importance and value of Christ's church would increase to the end that we would labor more for its unity, up-building, and outreach to the lost. And the voice of affirmation that we should seek the most comes not from the praise and accolades of men, but from that gracious expression given from the One who will one day say, *well done, good and faithful servant.*[199] In the end, we must be most invested in Christ's view of us above all.

Our calling as believers is to uphold the priorities of *Solus Christus* and *Sola Scriptura* as individuals and as Christ's body. We must therefore serve one another by subjecting ourselves to one another in the fear of Christ, magnifying His supremacy while guarding against any competitors to His office, whatever their popularity may be. As Christ's body we are to unfurl the banner of truth which He has entrusted to those who fear Him (Psalm 60:4), heralding a salvation that is by grace alone (*Sola Gratia*), through faith alone (*Sola Fide*) in Christ alone (*Solus Christus*), all for the glory of God alone (*Soli Deo Gloria*). In order to pursue this central mission of the church, we must seek to decrease so that Christ may increase in our individual lives, in our homes, in His church, and in this fallen world that needs Him so desperately. Dear brethren, let us serve one another in the *love, joy, and fear of our blessed Lord and Savior, Jesus Christ.*

---

[198] Revelation 1:17-20.

[199] Matthew 25:21.

MY
BANNER
IS
CHRIST

APPENDIX I

JOHN BUNYAN, JOHN FLAVEL

AND THE FEAR

OF GOD

Clearly, the subject of godly fear has proven to be of central importance to this work. By highlighting this doctrine, I readily admit that it was quite brief. I also must admit that, by stressing this subject, I did not offer a complete development of godly Christian affections. This was not unintentional. It was my goal to emphasize and undergird an important doctrine that has become nearly decimated in the modern day. Yet, the brevity of my treatment of this important subject makes me feel as though I have merely handed the reader a small cup of water out of a very deep well; after all, so much more can and should be said about the multifaceted subject of the fear of God. It is for this reason that, in the introduction of this book, I directed the reader's attention to the more thorough works of John Flavel and John Bunyan: *A Practical Treatise of Fear* and *A Treatise of the Fear of God*, respectively. As we have briefly observed, the works of these men were formulated within the crucible of significant trials whereby they learned that "it is far better to lose our carnal friends, estates, liberties, and lives, than part with Christ's truths and a good conscience."[200] Thus, this lesson was far more than a mere hypothesis to them in light of the religious opposition they faced. Admittedly, I only discovered their works quite recently, but upon reading them, I was richly blessed by both their lives and doctrine. In view of all this, I strongly urge the reader to take the time to partake of the rich writings of these men.

My own thoughts and concerns regarding the church's dangerous pattern of fearing and adoring men rather than God have been developing for many years. At the root of these concerns was a developing appreciation for the doctrine of the fear of God. Just as I was about to graduate from seminary, I began to spend a significant amount of time developing several papers in

---

[200] Flavel, <u>A Practical Treatise of Fear</u>, 303.

preparation for the ministry. While writing on the subject of the Gospel, I was especially struck by this text from John's Apocalypse:

> Revelation 14:6–7: 6 And I saw another angel flying in midheaven, having an eternal gospel to preach to those who live on the earth, and to every nation and tribe and tongue and people; 7 and he said with a loud voice, "Fear God, and give Him glory, because the hour of His judgment has come; and worship Him who made the heaven and the earth and sea and springs of waters."

What stood out for me in this passage is the redemptive mercy expressed in it, especially in light of the broader context of God's fierce judgment. As well, I was drawn by the fact that the angelic command to fear God, give Him glory, and worship Him is called *an eternal gospel.* John's use of the word *eternal* reminds us that, from the *protoevangelium* to the *Apocalypse,* God's decree of redemption is timeless and changeless. From this and many other passages, I continued to discover that the Scriptures are saturated with this subject of godly fear, and this is why it is quite surprising that the subject is rarely addressed. Sadly, the modern church has continued on a doctrinal path which has left this important doctrine in the dust of rationalism, subjectivism, liberalism, pragmatism, and emotionalism. To the extent that the church has continued to advocate a theology of irreverent faith,[201] it has resultantly mutilated the eternal Gospel's call to fear God, give

---

[201] As mentioned in the introduction, the use of the expression *irreverent faith* throughout this book points to the notion of a false faith which leads to irreverence and rebellion. True faith consists of a belief and trust that *God is* (Hebrews 11:6); is focused on the person and work of Jesus Christ (Acts 16:31); and yields the fruit of love, adoration, worship, and godly fear for Him as Lord and Savior (Revelation 14:6-7). It should be noted, however, that men and demons can have a form of faith which causes them to tremble at the sight of God (James 2:19), but such faith is shallow and devoid of true trust, love, adoration, and godly reverence.

Him glory, and worship Him. Yet, godly brethren throughout the ages have not avoided this important subject at all. We find that in Bunyan's work, *A Treatise of the Fear of God*, he addresses various aspects of godly and ungodly fear. I certainly found it interesting that he utilized Revelation 14:6-7 as the starting point for his multifaceted treatment of fear:

> FEAR GOD. — REVELATION 14:7: This exhortation is not only found here in the text, but is in several other places of the Scripture pressed, and that with much vehemency, upon the children of men, as in Ecclesiastes 12:13; 1 Peter 1:17, &c. I shall not trouble you with a long preamble, or forespeech to the matter, nor shall I here so much as meddle with the context, but shall immediately fall upon the words themselves, and briefly treat of the fear of God. The text, you see, presenteth us with a matter of greatest moment, to wit, with God, and with the fear of him. First they present us with God, the true and living God, maker of the worlds, and upholder of all things by the word of his power: that incomprehensible majesty, in comparison of whom all nations are less than the drop of a bucket, and than the small dust of the balance. This is he that fills heaven and earth, and is everywhere present with the children of men, beholding the evil and the good; for he hath set his eyes upon all their ways. So that, considering that by the text we have presented to our souls the Lord God and Maker of us all, who also will be either our Saviour or Judge, we are in reason and duty bound to give the more earnest heed to the things that shall be spoken, and be the more careful to receive them, and put them in practice; for, as I said, as they present us with the mighty God, so they exhort us to the highest duty towards him; to wit, to fear him. I call it the highest duty, because it is, as I may call it, not only a duty in itself, but, as it were, the salt that seasoneth every duty. For there is no duty performed by us that can by any means be accepted of God, if it be not seasoned with godly fear. Wherefore the apostle saith, 'Let us have grace, whereby we may serve God acceptably, with reverence and godly fear.'"[202]

---

[202] Bunyan, *A Treatise of the Fear of God*.

When Bunyan calls the fear of God the "salt that seasoneth every duty," he helps us to see the universality of reverence in relation to genuine faith and worship. Yet this fear does not come from the natural man, as Bunyan has already indicated: "No man brings this grace [godly fear] into the world with him. Everyone by nature is destitute of it; for naturally none fear God, there is no fear of God, none of this grace of fear before their eyes."[203] Just as the natural man is incapable of faith apart from grace, so it is the case that he is incapable of fear without that same, saving grace. To expand upon this important reality, Bunyan develops an eleven point analysis of the source of Godly fear:

"First. This fear, this grace of fear, this son- like fear of God, it flows from the distinguishing love of God to his elect. 'I will be their God,' saith he, 'and I will put my fear in their hearts.' None other obtain it but those that are enclosed and bound up in that bundle. Therefore they, in the same place, are said to be those that are wrapt up in the eternal or everlasting covenant of God, and so designed to be the people that should be blessed with this fear. 'I will make an everlasting covenant with them' saith God, 'that I will not turn away from them to do them good, but I will put my fear in their hearts, that they shall not depart from me' (Jer 32:38-40). This covenant declares unto men that God hath, in his heart, distinguishing love for some of the children of men; for he saith he will be their God, that he will not leave them, nor yet suffer them to depart, to wit, finally, from him. Into these men's hearts he doth put his fear, this blessed grace, and this rare and effectual sign of his love, and of their eternal salvation.

Second. This fear flows from a new heart. This fear is not in men by nature; the fear of devils they may have, as also an ungodly fear of God; but this fear is not in any but where there dwelleth a new heart, another fruit and effect of this everlasting covenant, and of this

---

[203] Ibid., 48.

distinguishing love of God. 'A new heart also will I give them' ; a new heart, what a one is that? why, the same prophet saith in another place, 'A heart to fear me,' a circumcised one, a sanctified one (Jer 32:39; Eze 11:19, 36:26). So then, until a man receive a heart from God, a heart from heaven, a new heart, he has not this fear of God in him. New wine must not be put into old bottles, lest the one, to wit, the bottles, mar the wine, or the wine the bottles; but new wine must have new bottles, and then both shall be preserved (Matt 9:17). This fear of God must not be, cannot be found in old hearts; old hearts are not bottles out of which this fear of God proceeds, but it is from an honest and good heart, from a new one, from such an one that is also an effect of the everlasting covenant, and love of God to men. 'I will give them one heart' to fear me; there must in all actions be heart, and without heart no action is good, nor can there be faith, love, or fear, from every kind of heart. These must flow from such a one, whose nature is to produce, and bring forth such fruit. Do men gather grapes of thorns, or figs of thistles? So from a corrupt heart there cannot proceed such fruit as the fear of God, as to believe in God, and love God (Luke 6:43-45). The heart naturally is deceitful above all things, and desperately wicked; how then should there flow from such an one the fear of God? It cannot be. He, therefore, that hath not received at the hands of God a new heart, cannot fear the Lord.

Third. This fear of God flows from an impression, a sound impression, that the Word of God maketh on our souls; for without an impress of the Word, there is no fear of God. Hence it is said that God gave to Israel good laws, statutes, and judgments, that they might learn them, and in learning them, learn to fear the Lord their God. Therefore, saith God, in another place, 'Gather the people together, men, and women, and children, and thy stranger that is within thy gates, that they may hear, and that they may learn and fear the Lord your God' (Deut 6:1,2, 31:12). For as a man drinketh good doctrine into his soul, so he feareth God. If he drinks it in much, he feareth him greatly; if he drinketh it in but little, he feareth him but little; if he drinketh it not in at all, he feareth him not at all. This, therefore, teacheth us how to judge who feareth the Lord; they are those that learn, and that stand in awe of the

Word. Those that have by the holy Word of God the very form of itself engraven upon the face of their souls, they fear God (Rom 6:17).[204] But, on the contrary, those that do not love good doctrine, that give not place to the wholesome truths of the God of heaven, revealed in his Testament, to take place in their souls, but rather despise it, and the true possessors of it, they fear not God. For, as I said before, this fear of God, it flows from a sound impression that the Word of God maketh upon the soul; and therefore,

Fourth. This godly fear floweth from faith; for where the Word maketh a sound impression on the soul, by that impression is faith begotten, whence also this fear doth flow. Therefore right hearing of the Word is called 'the hearing of faith' (Gal 3:2). Hence it is said again, 'By faith Noah, being warned of God of things not seen as yet, moved with fear, prepared an ark to the saving of his house, by the which he condemned the world, and became heir of the righteousness which is by faith' (Heb 11:7). The Word, the warning that he had from God of things not seen as yet, wrought, through faith therein, that fear of God in his heart that made him prepare against unseen dangers, and that he might be an inheritor of unseen happiness. Where, therefore, there is not faith in the Word of God, there can be none of this fear; and where the Word doth not make sound impression on the soul, there can be none of this faith. So that as vices hang together, and have the links of a chain, dependence one upon another, even so the graces of the Spirit also are the fruits of one another, and have such dependence on each other, that the one cannot be without the other. No faith, no fear of God; devil's faith, devil's fear; saint's faith, saint's fear.

Fifth. This godly fear also floweth from sound repentance for and from sin; godly sorrow worketh repentance, and godly repentance produceth this fear—'For behold,' says Paul, 'this self-same thing, that ye sorrowed

---

[204] Alas! how few attain to this most blessed state. To delight so in the Word—to make it so much our daily study, and the object of our meditations at night, as to have "its very form engraven upon the face of our souls." Happy is the man that is in such a case. O my soul, why is it not thy case?—Ed.

after a godly sort, what carefulness it wrought in you! yea, what clearing of yourselves! yea, what indignation! yea, what fear!' (2 Cor 7:10,11). Repentance is the effect of sorrow, and sorrow is the effect of smart,[205] and smart the effect of faith. Now, therefore, fear must needs be an effect of, and flow from repentance. Sinner, do not deceive thyself; if thou art a stranger to sound repentance, which standeth in sorrow and shame before God for sin, as also in turning from it, thou hast no fear of God; I mean none of this godly fear; for that is the fruit of, and floweth from, sound repentance.

Sixth. This godly fear also flows from a sense of the love and kindness of God to the soul. Where there is no sense of hope of the kindness and mercy of God by Jesus Christ, there can be none of this fear, but rather wrath and despair, which produceth that fear that is either devilish, or else that which is only wrought in us by the Spirit, as a spirit of bondage; but these we do not discourse of now; wherefore the godly fear that now I treat of, it floweth from some sense or hope of mercy from God by Jesus Christ— 'If thou, Lord,' says David, 'shouldest mark iniquities, O Lord, who shall stand? But there is forgiveness with thee that thou mayest be feared' (Psa 130:3, 4). 'There is mercy with thee'; this the soul hath sense of, and hope in, and therefore feareth God. Indeed nothing can lay a stronger obligation upon the heart to fear God, than sense of, or hope in mercy (Jer 33:8,9). This begetteth true tenderness of heart, true godly softness of spirit; this truly endeareth the affections to God; and in this true tenderness, softness, and endearedness of affection to God, lieth the very essence of this fear of the Lord, as is manifest by the fruit of this fear when we shall come to speak of it.

Seventh. This fear of God flows from a due consideration of the judgments of God that are to be executed in the world; yea, upon professors too. Yea further, God's people themselves, I mean as to themselves, have such a consideration of his judgments towards them, as to produce this godly fear. When God's judgments are in the earth,

---

[205] Sharp physical pain caused by a stroke, sting, or wound.

they effect the fear of his name, in the hearts of his own people— 'My flesh trembleth for fear of thee, and I am,' said David, 'afraid of thy judgments' (Psa 119:120). When God smote Uzzah, David was afraid of God that day (1 Chron 13:12). Indeed, many regard not the works of the Lord, nor take notice of the operation of his hands, and such cannot fear the Lord. But others observe and regard, and wisely consider of his doings, and of the judgments that he executeth, and that makes them fear the Lord. This God himself suggesteth as a means to make us fear him. Hence he commands the false prophet to be stoned, 'that all Israel might hear and fear.' Hence also he commanded that the rebellious son should be stoned, 'that all Israel might hear and fear.' A false witness was also to have the same judgment of God executed upon him, 'that all Israel might hear and fear.' The man also that did ought presumptuously was to die, 'that all Israel might hear and fear' (Deut 13:11, 21:21, 17:13, 19:20). There is a natural tendency in judgments, as judgments, to beget a fear of God in the heart of man, as man; but when the observation of the judgment of God is made by him that hath a principle of true grace in his soul, that observation being made, I say, by a gracious heart, produceth a fear of God in the soul of its own nature, to wit, a gracious or godly fear of God.

Eighth. This godly fear also flows from a godly remembrance of our former distresses, when we were distressed with our first fears; for though our first fears were begotten in us by the Spirit's working as a spirit of bondage, and so are not always to be entertained as such, yet even that fear leaveth in us, and upon our spirits, that sense and relish of our first awakenings and dread, as also occasioneth and produceth this godly fear. 'Take heed,' says God, 'and keep thy soul diligently, lest thou forget the things which thine eyes have seen, and lest they depart from thy heart all the days of thy life, but teach them thy sons, and thy son's sons.' But what were the things that their eyes had seen, that would so damnify them should they be forgotten? The answer is, the things which they saw at Horeb; to wit, the fire, the smoke, the darkness, the earthquake, their first awakenings by the law, by which they were brought into a bondage fear; yea, they were to remember this especially—'Specially,' saith he, 'the day that thou stoodest before the

Lord thy God in Horeb, when the Lord said unto me, Gather me the people together, and I will make them hear my words, that they may learn to fear me all the days that they shall live upon the earth' (Deut 4:9-11). The remembrance of what we saw, felt, feared, and trembled under the sense of, when our first fears were upon us, is that which will produce in our hearts this godly filial fear.

Ninth. This godly fear flows from our receiving of an answer of prayer, when we supplicated for mercy at the hand of God. See the proof for this—'If there be in the land famine, if there be pestilence, blasting, mildew, locust, or if there be caterpillar; if their enemy besiege them in the land of their cities, whatsoever plague, whatsoever sickness there be: what prayer and supplication soever be made by any man, or by all thy people Israel, which shall know every man the plague of his own heart, and spread forth his hands toward this house: then hear thou in heaven thy dwelling-place, and forgive, and do, and give to every man according to his ways, whose heart thou knowest (for thou, even thou only, knowest the hearts of all the children of men). That they may fear thee all the days of their life, that they live in the land which thou gavest unto our fathers' (1 Kings 8:37-40).

Tenth. This grace of fear also flows from a blessed conviction of the all-seeing eye of God; that is, from a belief that he certainly knoweth the heart, and seeth every one of the turnings and returnings thereof; this is intimated in the text last mentioned—"Whose heart thou knowest, that they may fear thee," to wit, so many of them as be, or shall be convinced of this. Indeed, without this conviction, this godly fear cannot be in us; the want of this conviction made the Pharisees such hypocrites—'Ye are they,' said Christ, 'which justify yourselves before men, but God knoweth your hearts' (Luke 16:15). The Pharisees, I say, were not aware of this; therefore they so much preferred themselves before those that by far were better than themselves, and it is for want of this conviction that men go on in such secret sins as they do, so much without fear either of God or his judgments.[206]

Eleventh. This grace of fear also flows from a sense of the impartial judgment of God upon men according to their works. This also is manifest from the text mentioned above. And give unto every man according to his works or ways, 'that they may fear thee,' &c. This is also manifest by that of Peter—'And if ye call on the Father, who without respect of persons judgeth according to every man's work, pass the time of your sojourning here in fear' (1Peter 1:17). He that hath godly conviction of this fear of God, will fear before him; by which fear their hearts are poised, and works directed with trembling, according to the will of God. Thus you see what a weighty and great grace this grace of the holy fear of God is, and how all the graces of the Holy Ghost yield mutually their help and strength to the nourishment and life of it; and also how it flows from them all, and hath a dependence upon every one of them for its due working in the heart of him that hath it."

We have much to learn from our Puritan forebears, and this small sample from Bunyan reminds us why this is so. The care and attention they gave to the study and application of the Scriptures is a much needed example for the modern day. Bunyan's aforementioned sources of godly fear offer some important building blocks for the doctrines of salvation, sanctification, and Christian affections. It is for this reason that this subject cannot be

---

[206] The filial fear of God is most prevalent when the heart is impressed with a lively sense of the love of God manifested in Christ. As a dutiful and obedient child fears to offend an affectionate parent, or as a person of grateful heart would be extremely careful not to grieve a kind and bountiful friend, who is continually loading him with favours and promoting his true happiness; so, and much more, will the gracious soul be afraid of displeasing the Lord, his bountiful and unwearied benefactor, who is crowning him with loving kindness and tender mercies.—Mason.

ignored. The absence of these truths has helped to create the fertile soils out of which the corruptions of celebritism and the fear of man have flourished. As already mentioned, *irreverence* is irreconcilable with *genuine faith and worship*. The sinner who believes that God *is*[207] and that He alone has the *awesome power and authority to forgive sin*[208] will, in faith, *do homage to the Son.*[209] These truths bring back to life the Gospel realities that have been buried for decades by shallow preaching. The average church member will be familiar with preaching that celebrates the broad and deep love of God *who so loved the world that He gave His only begotten Son (John 3:16a).* Yet fewer still will hear a peep about what it means *to perish without faith in the Son (John 3:16b).* Moreover, modern ears hear much from the 16th verse of John 3, but how many have heard a sermon on the 18th verse which reminds us that *those who do not believe in the Son have been judged already?*; or the 19th verse which teaches that *men love the darkness rather than the light for their deeds are evil?*; or the 36th verse which warns us that *he who does not believe in the Son will not see life, but the wrath of God abides on him?* These omissions are sadly common and remarkably dangerous. There is a sense in which the masses of the modern day have been called to a shallow and irreverent faith in an idol that can be identified as a savior, but is unworthy of being called Lord and Judge. This problem is not at all new. In his day, Bunyan had to refute those who argued that fear has no place in the Christian's life. Anticipating the arguments of his opponents, Bunyan addressed the text of 1 John 4:18 – a passage which is often mishandled by the opponents of godly fear:

> "Objection. But the Scripture says, 'perfect love casteth out fear' ; and therefore it seems that saints, after that a spirit of adoption is come,

---

[207] Hebrews 11:6.

[208] Psalm 130:4.

[209] Psalm 2:12.

should not fear, but do their duty, as another Scripture saith, without it (1 John 4:18; Luke 1:74,75).

Answer. Fear, as I have showed you, may be taken several ways. 1. It may be taken for the fear of devils. 2. It may be taken for the fear of reprobates. 3. It may be taken for the fear that is wrought in the godly by the Spirit as a spirit of bondage; or, 4. It may be taken for the fear that I have been but now discoursing of. Now the fear that perfect love casts out cannot be that son-like, gracious fear of God, that I have in this last place been treating of; because that fear that love casts out hath torment, but so has not the son-like fear. Therefore the fear that love casts out is either that fear that is like the fear of devils and reprobates, or that fear that is begot in the heart by the Spirit of God as a spirit of bondage, or both; for, indeed, all these kinds of fear have torment, and therefore may be cast out; and are so by the spirit of adoption, which is called the spirit of faith and love, when he comes with power into the soul; so that without this fear we should serve him. But to argue from these texts that we ought not to fear God, or to mix fear with our worship of him, is as much as to say that by the spirit of adoption we are made very rogues; for not to fear God is by the Scripture applied to such (Luke 23:40). But for what I have affirmed the Scripture doth plentifully confirm, saying, 'Happy is the man that feareth alway.' And again, 'It shall be well with them that fear God, which fear before him.' Fear, therefore; the spirit of the fear of the Lord is a grace that greatly beautifies a Christian, his words, and all his ways...”

Bunyan is consistent in reminding his readers of the fact that godly fear is a gift of God's grace and, as such, offers a sign of encouragement to those who have it and a warning to those who are found lacking:

“Is this fear of God such an excellent thing? Is it attended with so many blessed privileges? Then this should put us, every soul of us, upon a diligent examination of ourselves, to wit, whether this grace be in us or not, for if it be, then thou art one of these blessed ones to whom belong these glorious privileges, for thou hast an interest in every of them; but if it shall appear that this grace is not in thee, then thy state is fearfully miserable...”[210]

Bunyan's reminders and warnings are very important. If a physician regularly failed to warn his patients about the discovery of a fatal disease, he would lose his license to practice medicine; however, a different standard of practice is found in many churches today where the practitioners of modern ministry are actually celebrated for their dangerous lack of Gospel warnings. The sickness of sin has no cure other than the eternal Gospel of God. Those whose messages and examples of life promote a standard contrary to Christ's calling to lose one's life for His sake, will foster the dangerous and ungodly fear for one's life and self-preservation. John Flavel warns us against the dangers of these selfish affections:

“Our immoderate love of life, and the comforts and conveniences thereof, may be assigned as a proper, and real ground, and cause of our sinful fears, when the dangers of the times threaten the one or the other : did we love our lives less, we should fear and tremble less than we do. It is said of those renowned saints, Rev. xii. 11. " They overcame by the blood of the Lamb, and by the 'word of their testimony, and they loved not their lives unto the 'death.' They overcame not only the fury of their enemies without them, but their sinful fears within them ; and this victory was achieved by their mortification to the inordinate and immoderate love of life...This was it that freed Paul from slavish fears, and made him so magnanimous and undaunted...how did he attain so great courage and constancy of mind, in such deep and dreadful sufferings ! It was enough to have moved the stoutest man in the world, yea, and to have removed the resolutions of any that had not loved Christ better than his own life: but life was a trifle to him, in comparison with Jesus Christ, for so he tells us in the next words, 'I count not my life dear unto me,' It is a low-prized commodity in my

---

[210] Bunyan, *A Treatise of the Fear of God.*

eyes, not worth the saving, or regarding on such sinful terms. Oh ! how many have parted with Christ, peace, and eternal life, for fear of losing that which Paul regarded not. And if we bring our thoughts closer to the matter, we shall soon find that this is a fountain of fears in times of danger, and that from this excessive love of life we are racked and tortured with ten thousand terrors."[211]

A selfish, self-oriented fear leads us to a host of innumerable transgressions, as David teaches us: *do not fret; it leads only to evildoing (Psalm 37:8).* It is for this reason that the Devil continually revives ungodly fear in the hearts of men wherever he can. Flavel well exposes of Satan's tactic:

"I doubt not but it is a great design of the devil to keep us in continual alarms and frights, and to puzzle our heads and hearts with a thousand difficulties, which possibly may never befal us, or if they do, shall never prove so fatal to us as we fancy them, and all this is to unfit us for our present duties, and destroy our comfort therein ; for if by frights and terrors of mind he can but once distract our thoughts, he gains three points upon us to our unspeakable loss."[212]

In the fifth chapter, *Solus Christus in the Land of Sodom and Gomorrah,* we touched on the realities of the church's diminishing freedoms and possible persecution in coming days. Whatever our future, we must be prepared for the very battle to which God has called us. To do this, we must receive Paul's prescription and battle cry to *stand firm against the schemes of the Devil (Ephesians 6:11)* amidst our struggle against *the world forces of this darkness.* Armed with godly fear, we will hate evil, arrogance, and the evil way (Proverbs 8:13) and upheld by His strength, we can be ready as His soldiers, as Flavel reminds us:

---

[211] Flavel, <u>A Practical Treatise of Fear</u>, 268-69.
[212] Ibid., 272.

"Christianity is a warfare, and Christians must endure hardships, 2 Tim. ii. 3. Delicacy and tenderness is as odd a sight in a Christian, as it is in a soldier ; and we cannot be Christ's disciples, except we deliberate the terms, and having considered well what it is like to cost us, do resolve, in the strength of God, to run the hazard of all with him and for him. It is in vain to talk of a religion that we think not worthy the suffering and enduring any great matter for."[213]

Those who believe that the church's goal is to achieve friendship with the world under-cut the church's true calling of battle for the sake of the Gospel. Such battle compels us to rest in God's strength alone, without which we can do nothing:

"It is a great mistake to think that the mere strength of natural constitution, can carry any one through such sufferings for Christ, or that natural tenderness and weakness divinely assisted, cannot bear the heaviest burden that ever God laid upon the shoulders of any sufferer for Christ. Our suffering and bearing abilities are not from nature, but from grace. We find men of strong bodies and resolute daring minds, have fainted in the time of trial. Dr. Pendleton, in our own story, was a man of a robust and massy body, and a resolute daring mind; yet when he came to the trial, he utterly fainted and fell off. On the other side, what poor feeble bodies have sustained the greatest torments, and out of weakness have been made strong! Heb. xi. 34. The virgin Eulalia, of Emerita in Portugal, was young and tender, but twelve years old, and with much indulgence and tenderness brought up in an honourable family, being a person of considerable quality; yet how courageously did she sustain the most cruel torments for Christ! When the judge fawned upon her with this tempting language, 'Why wilt thou kill thyself, so young a flower,' and so near those honourable marriages and great dowries thou mightiest 'enjoy?' Instead of returning a retracting or double answer, Eulalia threw down the idol, and spurned abroad with her feet the heap of incense prepared for the censers; and when the executioner came to her, she entertained him with this language: 'Go to, thou hangman, burn, cut, mangle thou these earthly members; it is an easy matter to break a brittle substance, but the inward mind thou shalt not hurt.' And when one joint was pulled from another, she said, 'Behold what a pleasure it is for them, oh Christ! that remember thy triumphant victories, to attain unto those high dignities.' So that our constitutional strength is not to be made the measure of our passive fortitude: God can make the feeblest and tenderest persons stand, when strong bodies, and blustering, resolute, and daring minds faint and fall."[214]

Whatever challenges await the church, we can be sure that any such *sufferings of this present time are not worthy to be compared to the glory that is to be revealed (Romans 8:18)*; that *all things work together for good to those who love God, to those who are called according to His purpose (Romans 8:28)*; and our trials in this world are designed to show us the faithfulness of our heavenly Father who lovingly chastens His children so that they *may share His holiness (Hebrews 12:10)*. In all of this, it is our Lord's design is to have His people love, cherish, adore, fear, trust, and worship Him *alone*. In this we see the goodness of God in the darkest of days, or as Flavel says:

"Christians never find more kindness from God than when they feel most cruelty from men for his sake."[215]

Dear reader, may it be that we all would rest in His awesome power and kindness amidst this cruel and fallen world.

Soli Deo Gloria

---

[214] Ibid., 314-15.
[215] Ibid., 319.

MY
BANNER
IS
CHRIST

APPENDIX II

THE FEAR OF CHRIST

IN MARRIAGE

AND FAMILY

In the seventh chapter, *Solus Christus versus Man-centered Partisanship,* I mentioned some of the conflicts I faced early in my ministry with those who resisted the doctrines of grace as well as the Lordship of Christ in the salvation and sanctification of His people. This core problem produced the dangerous effect of hyper-grace teaching: a doctrine which utterly decimates the reality of God's perseverance of His people. As pressing as this conflict was, it was not the only challenge I faced at the time. During that same season of ministry, I faced another strong current of opposition dealing with the problem of what I now call *Evangelical Effeminism.* I used to refer to this same issue as *Evangelical Feminism,* but have come under the conviction that this is a slight misnomer. The reason why I say this is because the term *feminism, which depicts the sin of women rejecting their God ordained role* is merely a symptom of the greater disease of *effeminism: the sin of men rejecting their God ordained role to act and serve as leaders in the home, church, and world at large.* In other words, it is my conviction that feminism is the weed which thrives and depends on those sinful soils where men fail to *act like men*[216] and lead with Christ-like godliness. When men lead well as the heads of their households, the Savior is exalted, bringing peace and biblical order to their relationships with their wives and children. When they fail to lead, they foster rebellion and mayhem through the confusion of the biblical roles for men, women, children, and ultimately the church. If the leaders of a nation abandoned their posts, anarchy and unrest would surely be the result. And so it is for the family in which God calls the husband to serve as head: The man who fails to lead his home will produce a dangerous vacuum in which disorder will fester and grow. As for my early struggles and concerns with this issue, the more I saw

---

[216] 1 Corinthians 16:13: Be on the alert, stand firm in the faith, act like men, be strong.

evidences of feminism in the church and abroad, the more I noticed the presence of effeminate men who fostered such problems. For centuries, Satan has worked diligently to mass produce this disease in light of its caustic effects on the first of all institutions: marriage and family. Because of my increasing sense of alarm over the accelerated nature of this problem, I deliberated to produce my first book during those early years of ministry: *The First Institution – A Theological and Practical Guide for the Reformation of God's Institution of Marriage and Family.* While working on this project, I was struck by the doctrinal downgrade that has taken place within the church over the generations. What was once common theological knowledge has become alien thinking in the modern age. I was especially struck by this thought when reading Calvin's notes on 1 Timothy 2:12:

> *1 Timothy 2:12: But I suffer not a woman to teach.* Not that he takes from them the charge of instructing their family, but only excludes them from the office of teaching, which God has committed to men only. On this subject we have explained our views in the exposition of the First Epistle to the Corinthians. If any one bring forward, by way of objection, Deborah (Judges 4:4) and others of the same class, of whom we read that they were at one time appointed by the commend of God to govern the people, the answer is easy. Extraordinary acts done by God do not overturn the ordinary rules of government, by which he intended that we should be bound. Accordingly, if women at one time held the office of prophets and teachers, and that too when they were supernaturally called to it by the Spirit of God, He who is above all law might do this; but, being a peculiar case, this is not opposed to the constant and ordinary system of government.[217]

Upon reading this, I was impressed by the clarity of Calvin's instruction as well as his remarkable brevity in dealing with the

---

[217] Calvin, *Calvin's Commentaries.*

subject at hand. What was especially striking was the fact that Calvin was able to be brief because, in his day, few contested the plain teaching of Scripture on this subject. However, 150 years of Evangelical Effeminism's obscure interpretations of Scripture have made it quite difficult to respond only with simple answers. Our Puritan forebears did not have to confront such issues as we do now, and, if they could see the world of modern Evangelicalism today, I wonder if they would recognize it as being Christian at all. Satan's vicious onslaught against marriage and family only increases with time and it is for this reason that the church does not have the luxury of ignoring this assault. Manton was right when he said that the Devil seeks to supplant family duties in order to *crush the kingdom of Christ in the egg*. Moreover, decades of weak preaching on the subject of marriage and family have only increased Satan's agenda, and as a result our world has become a modern day Sodom and Gomorrah.

In the sixth chapter of this book, *Solus Christus in the Land of Sodom and Gomorrah*, we discussed the church's need to herald the Scriptures, while remembering that the world has become all the more hostile to the Lord and His authority. Thus, rather than shrinking back from controversial discussions about things like homosexuality and the institution of marriage, we should invite such conversations like a modern day Mars Hill debate for the sake of the Gospel. More personally, we must take heed unto ourselves by evaluating the integrity and dignity of our own marriages so that the Gospel will further prevail in our homes, our churches, and in the world at large. With this in mind, I would like to buttress and strengthen our understanding of the importance of marriage as an instrument by which we can communicate the Gospel to others. Much of this appendix is a summary from my book, *The First Institution*, with some distinctions. In this section, I will be addressing the relevancy and importance of godly fear as it relates to the institution of marriage. To do this, we will consider three points of analysis: *1. The Fear of Christ in the First Institution of Marriage; 2. The Fear of Christ in the Husband; 3. The Fear of Christ in the Wife; and 4. The Fear of Christ in the Home.* Our first category will address the need for godly fear in marriage in general:

1. The Fear of Christ in the First Institution of Marriage: Sadly, the word *marriage* has been kicked around like a football on an open field, but this is no game. Similar to the word rainbow, which has been co-opted by the advocates of homosexuality, the word marriage has been kidnapped and continues to be abused by our modern world. It is therefore important that we think carefully and reverently about God's decree of marriage as we have opportunity to engage others on this important subject. When we look at the Scriptures in their broadest view, *we find that the Bible begins and ends with the institution of marriage.* Yet, we must note that there is a vast difference between these two marital unions. In the book of Genesis we find that God created the earthly institution of marriage between Adam and his wife. Sadly, this union quickly descended into spiritual death through sin. However, we find that Scripture's second and final marital union comes in holiness and great victory, as seen in that heavenly vision given to the Apostle John:

> Revelation 19:6–8: 6 And I heard, as it were, the voice of a great multitude and as the sound of many waters and as the sound of mighty peals of thunder, saying, "Hallelujah! For the Lord our God, the Almighty, reigns. 7 "Let us rejoice and be glad and give the glory to Him, for the marriage of the Lamb has come and His bride has made herself ready." 8 And it was given to her to clothe herself in fine linen, bright and clean; for the fine linen is the righteous acts of the saints.

Though this stunning and climactic marriage scene is last in the Bible, it must not be last in our thoughts about God's purpose for this institution. From beginning to end, the Scriptures reveal God's plan to redeem a people of His choosing whom he would bring together in a marital union between the Lamb of God, Jesus Christ, and His bride, the church. Unlike temporal, earthly marriage, this marriage will endure forever without end. In a sense, the Bible's presentation of marriage moves from the lesser to the greater; from the temporal and corporeal to the spiritual and eternal. It is for this reason that we must calibrate our thinking about the word *marriage* in such a way that we remember God's decree of redemption and His purpose in the establishment of earthly marriage. It is this very redemptive-marital decree of God that is outlined in Paul's epistle to the Ephesians, whereby he describes the Father's choice of an elect people (Ephesians 1) who would be betrothed to the Son as prefigured in the institution of earthly marriage (Ephesians 5:22-33). It is in this important sense that, when we discuss marriage at all, we must subordinate our thoughts to that of the eternal union of Christ and His people:

> Ephesians 5:25–27: 25 Husbands, love your wives, just as Christ also loved the church and gave Himself up for her; 26 that He might sanctify her, having cleansed her by the washing of water with the word, 27 that He might present to Himself the church in all her glory, having no spot or wrinkle or any such thing; but that she should be holy and blameless.

Paul's instructions remind us that earthly marriage is a temporal shadow which directs our attention to the substance of Christ. It is for this reason that Paul directs his readers to pattern their marriages after the substance of Christ's union with His bride, the church. Should we think of marriage in any other way, we will demote its ultimate design. Bunyan reminds us of this important point: "This is one of God's chief ends in instituting marriage, that Christ and his church, under a figure, might be wherever there is a couple that believe through grace."[218] Thus, the Christian couple must remember that their marital union was designed by God to represent something far greater. Their union is to represent the Gospel truth concerning Christ's redemptive union with His people. This helps us to understand the truly *awesome,* or fear inspiring, nature of marriage. Too often discussions regarding marriage lack the heavenly perspective which God ordained. Such a habit as this demotes our perspective of marriage while degrading our thinking to fleshly and temporal levels. The result is that our view of marriage is degraded, *and our reverence for the Creator of this institution is dangerously weakened.* However, reverence for God and His word directs us to a right perspective of marriage. Since God designed earthly marriage to stand as a figure of the eternal marriage of Christ and His people, we must understand that this institution must be treated with great care and solemnity. The Lord has clearly expressed His holy hatred for the dissolution of His institution, *"' I hate divorce' says the Lord, the God of Israel..." (Malachi 2:16);* and Christ warned those who would dare destroy the marital union which God joins together, *"What therefore God has joined together, let no man separate."* It is crucial for us to understand that marriage is a very precious and important creation of our Lord. This is one of the reasons why godly fear is so needful for the preservation of the bonds of marriage, after all *the fear of the Lord is to hate evil (Proverbs 8:13).* Rather than treating marriage lightly, we should hate it when this institution is degraded or decimated by sin. One of the great dangers found within the church today is the growing sense of indifference towards divorce. Though we are right to be concerned about the rise of homosexuality, we are wrong to ignore the

---

[218] Bunyan, *Family Duty.*

rampant spread and acceptance of divorce. In view of this, it is crucial that husbands and wives reverence God and His decree of marriage. To the extent that couples herald the Lord's eternal institution of marriage, they will exercise better stewardship of its earthly figure. The wedding feast of the Lamb of God is the final consummation of our bridegroom's sacrificial work on our behalf. Jesus Christ, laid down His life for the church, rose again in power, and is returning again for His bride. As such, this is the one marital union that can never be dissolved because it will endure forever in holiness. *In the fear of Christ (Ephesians 5:21)*, husbands and wives must treat their marital unions with great appreciation and solemnity *(Ephesians 5:22-33)*.

2. The Fear of Christ in the Husband: When a man gives his marital vows to his bride, he makes a very grave commitment before God and men. The awesome responsibility that he assumes as a husband is this: he will serve and lead his wife as her head in the imitation of Christ in His love for the church.[219] Thus, godly fear is needful in view of this profound office, whereby the husband seeks to represent Christ in his home, as Bunyan says:

> "In a word, be such a husband to your believing wife, that she may say, God has not only given me a husband, but such a husband as preaches to me everyday the behavior of Christ to his church."[220]

The husband's calling is quite solemn, and it is for this reason that Bunyan also issues a serious warning to the man who fails to embrace His God-ordained role to serve in the imitation of Christ:

> "...that husband that carries himself indiscreetly towards his wife, he does not only behave himself contrary to the rule, but also makes his

---

[219] 1 Corinthians 11:3.
[220] Bunyan, *Family Duty.*

wife lose the benefit of such an ordinance, and crosses the mystery of his relation."[221]

In order for the husband to preach to his wife the behavior of Christ every day, he must pursue the heart and mind of Christ in the Scriptures. Rather than seeing his wife on the basis of cultural norms or natural impulses, he should view her in light of the Lord's valuation of her in the context of their marital union, and in view of the very love which led Christ to lay down His life for the church. When we think of Christ's sacrificial love, the first impulse is to consider His particular love for His people, however, there is an antecedent love that we must not miss. We are given a glimpse of this love between Christ's final Passover and His arrest in the Garden of Gesthemane:

> John 14:31: "but that the world may know that I love the Father, and as the Father gave Me commandment, even so I do. Arise, let us go from here... "

This expression of Christ's love for the Father was given between His betrayal by Judas (John 13) and His crucifixion at Golgotha (John 19). Thus, Christ's call to the disciples to *arise* and *go* with Him was an invitation to join Him on a pathway that would lead to His arrest, trial, and eventual death. John 14:31 helps our understanding regarding the heart and mind of Christ, *especially in view of the message of love which He wanted the world to know.* This is crucial because, when we think of the nature of Christ's sacrificial love, our thoughts tend to gravitate towards the savior's affections for the church. While wonderfully important, this does not constitute His foremost affection. John 14:31 gives us an important understanding of the Savior's principal love for, and obedience to, the Father which ultimately led Him to the cross. As

---

[221] Ibid.

well, this passage reminds us that Christ, who is the fulfillment of the law, is the greatest example of the foremost commandment of love.[222] The Father and Son have forever abided, *face to face (pros ton theon)*,[223] in this mutual bond of love, and this same love will abide forever without end.[224] Ultimately, if we are to consider the husband's imitation of Christ, he must first consider Christ's own priority of love. Christ's first love was not the church, and His motive of sacrificial obedience was not established by any man-centeredness. Instead, His love for the Father established the centerpiece for His love for the church. Thus, if a man's love for his wife is not grounded in this priority of a love for God *first and foremost*, then his affections will become sinfully corrupted. His tendency will be to exalt the creature rather than the creator, heralding his wife, himself, or his children above the Lord Himself. The graveyard of human history is sadly littered with marital unions which perished because love for Christ did not reign supreme. However, when a husband loves and reverences the Lord *first*, he will enjoy the blessings of the promise: "...I will put the fear of Me in their hearts so that they will not turn away from Me" Jeremiah 32:40). The man who loves, reverences, and cherishes the Lord will also love and cherish the gifts that He gives. It is for this reason that the man who lives out a loving fidelity to Christ will also live out a loving fidelity to his wife.

The Lord's love for His bride is a unique and particular love. It is not to be equated to His general love for mankind which is an

---

[222] Mark 12:28-31.

[223] "And the Word was face to face with God (*pros ton theon*). The meaning is that the Word existed in the closest possible fellowship with the father, and that he took supreme delight in this communion." William Hendriksen, New Testament Commentary, The Gospel of John (Grand Rapids: Baker Book House), 70.

[224] John 17:22-26.

212

expression of His common grace.[225] God's relationship with His people is established on the basis of knowledge, spiritual intimacy, and a personal relationship:

> Hosea 2:19–20: 19 "And I will betroth you to Me forever; Yes, I will betroth you to Me in righteousness and in justice, In lovingkindness and in compassion, 20 And I will betroth you to Me in faithfulness. *Then you will know the LORD.* (italics mine).

As well, He disdains shallowness and indifference, but delights in a genuine love and loyalty from those who are His:

> Hosea 6:6 "...I delight in loyalty rather than sacrifice, And in the knowledge of God rather than burnt offerings."

Sadly, many today teach that marital love is little more than the *neighbor love* mentioned in the foremost commandment (Mark 12:31), but is only distinguished by sexual intimacy. This is a remarkably horrible concept which offers an over-simplification of scriptural teaching. In fact, one of the pastors mentioned in the sixth chapter, *Solus Christus in the Home and Church,* who fell to sexual sin, taught this very doctrine. Not only did *he* teach it, but other prominent men who were influences in his life teach it as well. One can hardly imagine a man telling his neighbor that his love for others is no different than his love for his wife, *save the bedroom.* Such teaching enters into rank hedonism and relational indifference, the likes of which will certainly lead to ruin. Yet, the scriptural standard reminds us that the husband who imitates God's marital love for His people, will *love and know his wife* well enough to minister to her spiritual needs (Ephesians 5:26) as well as her physical needs (Ephesians 5:28-30). Such personal knowledge of her will mean that his parental leadership in the

---

[225] Matthew 5:43-45.

home (Ephesians 6:4) will be well buttressed through her familiar ministry as his helpmeet (Ephesians 6:1-3). Moreover, he will know her well enough to minister grace and compassion to her in light of her unique frailties as a woman:

> 1 Peter 3:7: You husbands likewise, live with your wives in an understanding way, as with a weaker vessel, since she is a woman; and grant her honor as a fellow heir of the grace of life, so that your prayers may not be hindered.

The husband who serves as the head and leader of his wife is to honor and love her with a deep understanding of her uniqueness as a creation and gift of God. He must also love and honor her in view of her particular frailties so that he can extend to her the grace of compassion in view of her needs. However, the man who is relationally indifferent to his wife won't care for such knowledge and will relate to her without such compassion. Peter's overall teaching in 1 Peter 3:1-7 reminds us that the godly husband will seek a relational love with his wife and treat her accordingly; but the indifferent husband ignores God's instructions as well as his wife's needs and, by such sin, will have his prayers hindered. Peter's description of the wife being a *fellow heir of the grace of life* reminds the husband that he and she both share the frailty of sin; that they are needy recipients of grace; and that they are to minister to each other in the fear of Christ.[226] Rather than carrying on in ignorance and indifference, the husband must confess that

---

[226] Peter's use of the word grace in the expression fellow heir of the grace of life reminds the godly husband where he stands in his marital union. His calling to be the head of his home does not make him superior to his wife. Rather, he and his wife both stand at the foot of the cross as the recipients of forgiveness so that the Lord may be feared (Psalm 130:4, Ephesians 5:21). As the equal recipients of grace, they are to minister love and compassion to one another in view of their respective roles established by the Lord's authority.

he has a great and continual need to learn about how he is to love and minister to his wife:

> "Christ laid out his life for his church, covers her infirmities, communicates to her his wisdom, protects her, and helps her in her employments in this world; and so should men do for their wives...Therefore bear with their weaknesses, help their infirmities, and honor them as the weaker vessels, and as being of a frailer constitution (1 Peter 3:7)."[227]

Christ's marital love for the church supplies the crucial model for the husband. By His example, the husband must remember that love for God formulates the centerpiece of his love for his wife. As well, the Lord's design is that marital love would be *uncommon*, being distinguished by a personal union and knowledge between the bridegroom and his bride. This is much more than sexual intimacy; it is a spiritual union and relationship which should only come second to their relationship with the Lord Himself. So it is with Christ and His people, and so it should be between a believing husband and wife. The husband who understands the *awesome* nature of his calling will *rejoice with trembling* in the *fear of Christ.*

3. The Fear of Christ in the Wife: The wife's duty to serve in the fear of Christ is certainly no less than that of her husband's. Together, they both are called to the awesome task of representing Christ's union with His people, each according to their role. The husband is to model Christ in His sacrificial love for, and leadership of, the church. The wife is to model the church by means of loving submission:

---

[227] Bunyan, *Family Duty.*

Ephesians 5:21–33: 21 and be subject to one another in the fear of Christ. 22 Wives, be subject to your own husbands, as to the Lord. 23 For the husband is the head of the wife, as Christ also is the head of the church, He Himself being the Savior of the body. 24 But as the church is subject to Christ, so also the wives ought to be to their husbands in everything. 25 Husbands, love your wives, just as Christ also loved the church and gave Himself up for her; 26 that He might sanctify her, having cleansed her by the washing of water with the word, 27 that He might present to Himself the church in all her glory, having no spot or wrinkle or any such thing; but that she should be holy and blameless. 28 So husbands ought also to love their own wives as their own bodies. He who loves his own wife loves himself; 29 for no one ever hated his own flesh, but nourishes and cherishes it, just as Christ also does the church, 30 because we are members of His body. 31 FOR THIS CAUSE A MAN SHALL LEAVE HIS FATHER AND MOTHER, AND SHALL CLEAVE TO HIS WIFE; AND THE TWO SHALL BECOME ONE FLESH. 32 This mystery is great; but I am speaking with reference to Christ and the church. 33 Nevertheless let each individual among you also love his own wife even as himself; and let the wife see to it that she respect her husband.

Contextually speaking, Paul's description of the church's mutual servanthood and subjection in Ephesians 5:21 is qualified by a series of important instructions in Ephesians 5:22-6:9. He makes it quite clear that the church's mutual subjection and servanthood does not nullify the distinctive roles of leadership and servitude among husbands and wives (Ephesians 5:22-33); parents and children (Ephesians 6:1-4); and servants and masters (Ephesians 6:5-9). Without such distinctions, erroneous conclusions would certainly flow from a faulty understanding of Ephesians 5:21, which Evangelical Effeminism/Feminism has promoted *ad nauseam*. More will be said about this at the end of this section, but it is sufficient to note that Paul's description of the body's universal subjection and servitude does not eliminate the unique submission that a wife is to offer to her husband within the bond of marital love. Grammatically speaking, the participle given in Ephesians 5:21 (*being subject - ʹupotassomenoi*) supplies the elliptical thought in verse 22 and is restated in verse 24:

Ephesians 5:22: 22 Wives, *be subject* to your own husbands, as to the Lord.

Ephesians 5:24: 24 But as [*ŏs*] the church is subject [*upotassetai*] to Christ, so also the wives *ought to be* to their husbands in everything.

Elliptical constructions are common in the Scriptures and they are easily identified in Bible translations in the form of italicized words and expressions.[228] In connection with this, verse 24 clearly shows that Paul is making a comparison [*ŏs*][229] between the church's submission unto Christ and the wife's submission to her husband: "so also the wives *ought to be [i.e., ought to be submissive - upotassetai]* to their husbands in everything." Despite the creative efforts of feminists today, Paul's call for the submission of wives to their husbands is without dispute. The Christian home is not a leaderless place abounding in anarchy, but is a place where the husband is to serve *by leading his wife,* and the wife is to serve *by submitting to her husband.* Calvin is quite right when he says that "...wives cannot obey Christ without yielding obedience to their husbands."[230] These role distinctions must neither be ignored nor confused since it is the Christian couple's duty to imitate Christ's union with His people. This calling of theirs *is an important and fearful one* such that the neglect of it brings forth severe consequences:

---

[228] Paul's epistle to the Ephesians begins with an elliptical construction in Ephesians 1:3: "Blessed *be* the God and Father of our Lord Jesus Christ..."

[229] Paul's use of the comparative particle *ŏs* establishes the relationship of thought between the church and wives.

[230] Calvin, *Calvin's Commentaries.*

MY BANNER IS CHRIST

> Titus 2:3–5: 3 Older women likewise are to be reverent in their
> behavior, not malicious gossips, nor enslaved to much wine, teaching
> what is good, 4 that they may encourage the young women to love their
> husbands, to love their children, 5 to be sensible, pure, workers at
> home, kind, being subject to their own husbands, *that the word of God
> may not be dishonored.* [italics mine].

Paul's emphasis on the duties of a wife carries with it a grave
warning at the end of verse 5. The word that he uses, represented
by the NASB's choice of *dishonored*, is quite strong: *blasphēmētai
– blasphemed.* Through this warning, Paul helps us to see the
gravity of the wife's distinctive role in the home and before a
watching world. Should she honor her role, she brings forth the
blessed example of the church's joyful and loving submission to
her husband, Jesus Christ. Should she deny her role, she literally
blasphemes God and His word. In view of this, her ministry in the
home must be carried out in the fear of Christ understanding that
her children need to hear the Gospel and even see it being
previewed by the father and the mother.

Women today are repeatedly being told that they must consider
the idea of submission as abject slavery and a form of abuse from
ancient history. This Satanic message continues to be spread
within contemporary Christianity, giving rise to all forms of
corruption and blasphemy against God's word. However, the Lord
has said that he delights in the imperishable quality of a gentle and
quiet spirit, *one which renders joyful submission to the husband:*

> 1 Peter 3:3–6: 3 And let not your adornment be merely external—
> braiding the hair, and wearing gold jewelry, or putting on dresses;4 but
> let it be the hidden person of the heart, with the imperishable quality of
> a gentle and quiet spirit, which is precious in the sight of God. 5 For in
> this way in former times the holy women also, who hoped in God, used

to adorn themselves, being submissive to their own husbands. 6 Thus Sarah obeyed Abraham, calling him lord, and you have become her children if you do what is right without being frightened by any fear

When Peter penned his epistles, he wrote to a people who lived beneath a vastly different system of civil law and ethics. Adultery committed by a husband was often viewed as acceptable, whereas a wife would be deemed guilty without question.[231] The father's authority over all property and life within the home was such that he could, in some cases, hasten the death of a family member with very little jurisprudence. These civil standards would change within a half century, but to his immediate readers the reality of suffering under harsh conditions was quite real.[232] But Peter exhorted them to remain faithful to the Lord despite the standards of Roman law and government. Peter clearly articulated to his readers that they may even suffer in the process, but their focus must be to suffer for righteousness sake rather than for doing evil. In the case of a wife, whose husband was being disobedient to the Word (1 Peter 3:1), Peter did not retract the call of submission, but

---

[231] "In Roman law up to the time of the Republic the husband has, in a case of adulterium, the one-sided right of private revenge against the guilty wife even to putting to death, whereas the wife must accept the adultery of her husband." ." Kittel, Gerhard, Geoffrey William Bromiley, and Gerhard Friedrich, Theological Dictionary of the New Testament.Vol. 2, ed. (Grand Rapids, MI, 1964-c1976), Vol. 4, 471.

[232] Will Durant affirms that Roman law did change during the reign of Emperor Hadrian (A.D. 117-138): "The second person in Roman law was the father...Rule through family and clan diminished as population became more abundant and diverse, and life more mobile, commercial, and complex; kinship, status, and custom were replaced by contract and law. Children won greater freedom from their parents, wives from their husbands, individuals from their groups. Trajan compelled a father to emancipate a son whom he had maltreated; Hadrian took from the father the right of life and death over his household and transferred it to the courts." Will Durant, The Story of Civilization: Part III, Caesar and Christ (New York: Simon and Schuster), 395.

instead he underscored the importance of her need to fear God rather than men, after the pattern of Sarah. Peter's instruction to the wife is in no way new, for it reflects the very call from the Lord to fear Him above all.[233] These commands may seem very distant and strange to an age of self-esteem, self-awareness, self-image, and self-preservation. Clearly, Satan's temptation to women has not changed since the beginning, and he continues to provoke ungodly fear within women, whispering in their ear that they may not have all that they could possess should they remain committed to obeying God's commands. Modern counseling models tend to prey on women who are weighed down by man-centered fears,[234] offering them sham solutions to very real problems by offering the false promise that our lives can be sterilized of all suffering. But godly women of every era are to forsake worldly fear and resist the Devil while placing their hope in the Creator who made them and redeemed them by the blood of the Lamb.[235] In an age that exalts self-esteem and self-preservation, fleshly fears are often catered to in a manner that forsakes Peter's serious exhortation to godliness. This apostolic teaching must not be missed nor ignored, for *what is more important than one's self-preservation is the upholding of a godly witness in a fallen world.* Ultimately, such selflessness comes from a heart that ministers in the fear of Christ. Such godly fear within the wife is consistent with her imitation of the church's reverence for Christ:

---

[233] Matthew 10:28 "And do not fear those who kill the body, but are unable to kill the soul; but rather fear Him who is able to destroy both soul and body in hell."

[234] 2 Timothy 3:6-7: 6 For of this sort are those who creep into households and make captives of gullible women loaded down with sins, led away by various lusts,7 always learning and never able to come to the knowledge of the truth.

[235] 1 Peter 1:3 Blessed be the God and Father of our Lord Jesus Christ, who according to His great mercy has caused us to be born again to a living hope through the resurrection of Jesus Christ from the dead.

Ephesians 5:33 Nevertheless let every one of you in particular so love his wife even as himself; and the wife see that she reverence [*phobētai*] her husband. [KJV]

In imitation of the church at its best, the wife is to minister to her husband in godly reverence/fear. As already stated throughout this book, this is not ungodly fear, but the godly fear which has at its center an adoration and appreciation of the Lord above all. Thus, the wife's reverence for her husband is an expression of respect, appreciation, and submission in view of the husband's role as her head in the imitation of Christ. Clearly, Paul is not instructing wives to *be afraid* of their husbands, but to have and demonstrate a profound respect for them in view of the Lord's ordaining the husband to serve as her headship. Clearly, the act of submitting to imperfect leadership can be, humanly speaking, a fearful prospect, whether to a wicked king, a ruler, or a husband; but the woman who fears God will submit to her husband with full trust and confidence *in the Lord*.

4. The Fear of Christ in the Home: From what we have considered thus far, it is quite clear that the husband and wife have a very significant ministry through their calling to imitate Christ and the church. In the broadest sense, the believing couple's marital ministry constitutes a significant testimony to the lost of this world who have yet to hear of the Lord's unique love for His people in the message of the Gospel. Within the home, this same ministry constitutes the foundation of the parent's relationship with their children. Through the piety of their lives and integrity of their doctrine, the believing couple will render the fragrant aroma of Christ in the home. However, the absence of such piety and doctrine renders the putrefying stench of hypocrisy. Thus, God's ministry of the word in the home is a very serious matter to consider for any generation. The continuity of Paul's instructions throughout Ephesians 5:22-6:4 makes it clear that God's design for the family is this: Children are to receive more than a verbal presentation of the Gospel - they need to see marriage as the figure of Christ's loving relationship with His church. Such a ministry in the home has no ecclesiastical substitute and it is for this reason that fathers and mothers are not free to abandon their Gospel duties to surrogate individuals or programs within the church. As long as they have life and breath, they have a continual responsibility to herald Christ and the Gospel before their children. They are to do this in the fear of Christ, while their children are to obey and honor their parents:

> Ephesians 6:1–3: 1 CHILDREN, obey your parents in the Lord, for this is right. 2 HONOR YOUR FATHER AND MOTHER (which is the first commandment with a promise), 3 THAT IT MAY BE WELL WITH YOU, AND THAT YOU MAY LIVE LONG ON THE EARTH.

Paul's instructions to children are fairly simple: they are to *obey* and *honor* their parents. Yet, we must wonder what is assumed about the spiritual station of these children from what he writes. Is Paul writing to the church under the assumption that all the children are believers, or does he write with the assumption that there will be a mixture of believers and unbelievers? I would suggest that Paul's recitation of the 5th commandment connotes a broader audience,[236] one which required a *lawful tutelage* which leads unbelievers to Christ,[237] and one which exhorts believers to pious living. Paul alludes to this same lawful tutelage when he wrote to Timothy, reminding him that from his youth he had

---

[236] Paul's instructions in Col 3:18-21 are far more generic and therefore comport with the breadth of application of discipleship and Gospel appeal. A child's obedience to their parents is an opportunity for discipleship as well as a Gospel appeal.

[237] Gal 3:24.

known the sacred writings which were able to give him the wisdom that leads to salvation (2 Timothy 3:14-15). Being exposed to the law from his youth[238] Timothy was blessed with the very Scriptures which lead us to our need for Christ:

> Galatians 3:24: Therefore the Law has become our tutor to lead us to Christ, that we may be justified by faith.

Paul's introduction of the law comports with what we would expect within a spiritual household[239] with children of any age or station. As the Lord blesses a family with children, the labor of the Gospel prevails through the primitive tutelage of the law, and through the discipleship of children who come to faith. Thus, Paul has not missed anyone in Ephesians 6:1-3. Paul's instruction explicitly teaches that all children are called to submit to the spiritual tutelage of their parents: believing children are thus called out of their spiritual ability to do so as unto the Lord,[240] and unbelieving children must be tutored in the same submission in order to expose their spiritual inability and need for Christ.[241]

As we further consider Paul's command that children honor their parents, we find that this instruction reveals the importance of a child's valuation of their father and mother. Paul's injunction in

---

[238] For an extended treatment of Timothy's training from his youth [*brephos*], even as it relates to evangelism in the home, see *The First Institution*, pp. 218-226.

[239] In the broadest sense, a spiritual household is one that possesses the Gospel influence of one or more believers (2 Tim. 1:5; 3:14-15). According to Paul, the presence of a believing spouse, within any family, sanctifies it (sets it apart) by the presence of God's grace, the Holy Spirit, and the Gospel (1 Cor. 7:14). This does not mean that unbelievers are thereby saved by such an influence; nor does it mean that they will ever be saved; but the believer's association does distinguish the family, spiritually, by means of God's presence within the believer.

[240] Eph. 6:1.

[241] Eph. 2:8-9, 6:2-3.

Ephesians 6:2-3 reveals that parents are to be held in high regard as being the very representatives of the Lord Himself. When we consider the broader significance and meaning of *honor*, we understand that it is one of the chief components of love and respect, after all, brethren are to show honor to one another (Romans 12:10); the husband is to honor his wife (1 Peter 3:7); wives are to honor and respect their husbands (Ephesians 5:33); and we are to honor all men including those who are in governing authority (1 Peter 2:17). The act of honoring others is a significant part of the Christian life and it is to be one of the earliest lessons impressed upon children. Paul taught this principle by drawing from the Old Testament Scriptures:

> **Exodus 20:12** Honor your father and your mother, that your days may be prolonged in the land which the Lord your God gives you.

> **Deuteronomy 5:16** Honor your father and your mother, as the Lord your God has commanded you, that your days may be prolonged, and that it may go well with you on the land which the Lord your God gives you.

Like many Old Testament conditional statements, the fifth commandment is not necessarily *guaranteeing* longevity for obedient children, but it does describe the blessings of life that often attend children who respect and honor their parents. The crucial concept here is this: children are safest in this life when they readily subject themselves to the protective care and covering of their parents. This stands in opposition to the child who dishonors his parents by rejecting discipline and instruction. A rebellious child who dishonors and rejects parental tutelage is choosing to live outside of the umbrella of God's ordained protection. What we learn from this instruction to children is this important truth: parents are a gift from God to their children! This is essentially the mirrored truth of the teaching found in Psalm 127 where we see that children are *a gift of the Lord*. What the scriptures repeatedly teach us is that God Himself is exalted *and honored* when we give Him thanks for His various gifts to us: children to parents; parents to children, a husband to a wife, or a wife to a husband. Adam modelled this when the Lord gave him the gift of his wife:

> Genesis 2:22-23: 22 And the LORD God *fashioned* into a woman the rib which He had taken from the man, and *brought* her to the man. And the man said, "This is now bone of my bones, and flesh of my flesh; She shall be called Woman, because she was taken out of Man." (italics mine).

Everything in this scene points to the goodness of God's gifts, after all, the Lord declared that all He had made was *very good* (Genesis 1:31). Adam recognized this goodness of God's handiwork, acknowledging that she was bone of his bones, flesh of his flesh for she was taken out of man. After the fall, such gratitude and honor became utterly alien to the natural heart:

> Romans 1:21: For even though they knew God, they did not *honor* Him as God, or *give thanks*; but they became futile in their speculations, and their foolish heart was darkened. (italics mine)

It is for this reason that children are to be regularly shown the scriptural mandate of honoring their parents, yet to the higher end of honoring the One who gave them their parents in the first place. Such relationships of honor have a point and purpose, and it is this: The chief end is that God would be honored in all things (Malachi 1:6).

Malachi 1:6 A son honors his father, and a servant his master. Then if I am a father, where is My honor? And if I am a master, where is My respect? says the Lord of hosts...

The supreme point of honoring others is so that we would honor the Lord who is above all. It is in this sense that the call of obedience to the fifth commandment provides the primitive tutelage which ultimately points to God's deserved honor and glory as expressed in the *eternal Gospel: "fear God, and give Him glory, because the hour of His judgment has come; worship Him who made the heaven and the earth and sea and the springs of water"* (Revelation 14:6-7). This is the central calling of parents towards their children: to minister the Gospel to their children to the end that they would know, love, reverence, and honor the Lord who is the Savior, Judge, and the Creator of the heavens and the earth. Such is the privilege and duty of every home that ministers in the fear of Christ, and such an environment as this is the death knell to all the idols and stumbling blocks of this world.

As a final point of consideration, I will add some points of observation concerning the meaning and application of Ephesians 5:21 ["...and be subject to one another in the fear of Christ"], especially since this text has been so central to this book. As already noted, the Apostle Paul's important instructions regarding marriage in Ephesians 5:22-33 cannot be fully understood apart from the broader context of the chapter overall. In a sense, Paul's argument grows and develops like a tree, beginning with the root and extending to various branches of piety in the church and in the home. Thus, to comprehend the context of the latter portion of the chapter, we must also consider its beginning – *its root: Ephesians 5:1-2 1 Therefore be imitators of God, as beloved children; 2 and walk in love, just as Christ also loved you and gave Himself up for us, an offering and a sacrifice to God as a fragrant aroma.* Paul's root instruction is established by two imperatives: *be imitators* (of God) and *walk* (in love). By beginning with these commands, Paul orients our thinking about what kind of love we are to imitate. Clearly, it is not the selfish, hedonistic "love" of the Greco-Roman world, but is the relational love of God as revealed in the person and work of Jesus Christ *who loved us and gave Himself up for us, an offering and a sacrifice to God as a fragrant aroma.* This latter command given by Paul *to walk in love, after the pattern of Christ's humble servitude,* then branches out to two additional commands of pious, Christ-like living: *Ephesians 5:8 ...walk as children of light,* and *Ephesians 5:15-16 15 be careful how you walk, not as unwise men but as wise, 16 making the most of your time because the days are evil.* After this repeated instruction to walk in godliness, Paul then adds four additional injunctions to pious living: *1. Do not be foolish (v. 17a); 2. but understand what the will of the Lord is (v. 17b); 3. Do not get drunk with wine (v. 18a); 4. Be filled [plērousthē] with the Spirit (v. 18b).* As the grammatical tree expands and fills the page, Paul then issues five participles which describe what Spirit-filled living looks like: *1. Speaking [lalountes] to one another in psalms and hymns and spiritual songs, 2. Singing [adontes] and 3. making melody [psallontes] with your heart to the Lord, 4. always giving thanks [eucharistountes] for all things in the name of our Lord Jesus Christ to God, even the Father, 5. Subjecting yourselves [upotassomenoi] to one another in the fear of Christ [en phobō Christou].* Clearly, the fear of Christ is a gift of grace, wrought by the Spirit who fills the believer (Ephesians 5:18). Such reverential servitude provides an important staging point for his instructions to wives who are called to submit themselves to their husbands (Ephesians 5:22-24, 33); to husbands who are called to subject themselves to a Christ-like servitude and leadership (Ephesians 5:25-33); to children who are to be in subjection to their parents (Ephesians 6:1-4), to servants who are to obey in fear and trembling *as to Christ* (Ephesians 6:5-8), and to masters who are commanded to kindness in view of the sovereign authority of their Master, Jesus Christ (Ephesians 6:5-9). Paul's mention of being subject to one another *in the fear of Christ* supplies a crucial stage of thought in which he reminds us of the supremacy and Lordship of Christ over His church. The relationship between Ephesians 5:21 to what precedes and what follows is central to this core lesson: No member of Christ's body possesses personal or inherent authority, instead, our ordained roles are given to us by Christ who is the Lord and head of the Church:

> Ephesians 1:20–23: 20 ...He [the Father] raised Him from the dead, and seated Him at His right hand in the heavenly places, 21 far above all rule and authority and power and dominion, and every name that is named, not only in this age, but also in the one to come. 22 And He put all things in subjection [*upetaxen*][242] under His feet, and gave Him as head over all things to the church, 23 which is His body, the fullness of Him who fills all in all.

Paul only uses the word *upotassō* three times in Ephesians: twice in the fifth chapter (as already observed) and once in the first chapter (as above). The continuity of his argument is quite clear. All authority belongs to Christ and therefore He rules as the Lord of lords over all authority, power, and dominion. As well, Christ has all authority over the church and therefore all things are *subject* to him *because he is the head of His bride.* Paul's emphasis on Christ's absolute authority renders the piercing reminder that no creature can, or ever will, possess any *inherent authority.* It is for this reason that even kings and governors must see themselves as servants of man and God in view of the absolute sovereignty of Christ, as Calvin observes:

---

[242] 3rd person singular, aorist active indicative of *upotassō*.

"God has bound us so strongly to each other, that no man ought to endeavor to avoid subjection; and where love reigns, mutual services will be rendered. I do not except even kings and governors, whose very authority is held for the *service* of the community. It is highly proper that all should be exhorted to be subject to each other in their turn."[243]

Such mutual subjection is not an abrogation of our respective roles in life, as ordained by Christ, but instead denotes an attitude of humility and servitude *in the fear of Christ and His absolute authority over us all*. Matthew Henry offers us important words of wisdom on this matter:

There is a mutual submission that Christians owe one to another, condescending to bear one another's burdens: not advancing themselves above others, nor domineering over one another and giving laws to one another. Paul was an example of this truly Christian temper, for he *became all things to all men*. We must be of a yielding and of a submissive spirit, and ready to all the duties of the respective places and stations that God has allotted to us in the world. [244]

We do have *respective places and stations that God has allotted to us in the world,* and we must carry out these places and stations *being subject to one another in the fear of Christ.* The calling of a husband to lead as the head of his home comes not from himself, but from the Lord; The wife who is called to serve as the helpmeet to her husband does so on the basis of Christ's authority, not her own; and, again, the calling of parents to teach and nurture their children comes by the authority of Christ, and not they themselves. Such reminders as these place all the members of Christ's body in the proper place of submissive servitude before Christ who is the head of the church.

---

[243] Calvin, *Calvin's Commentaries.*

[244] Matthew Henry, *Matthew Henry's commentary on the whole Bible: Complete and unabridged in one volume* (Peabody: Hendrickson, 1994), 2317.

In all of these instructions, Paul is commanding *all members of the church* to walk after the pattern of Christ who came, not to be served, but to serve, and to give His life a ransom for many (Matthew 20:28). This brings us to the important transition from verse 21 to 22. As already noted, Ephesians 5:21 supplies the last in a series of five participles which describe what Spirit-filled living looks like: *Ephesians 5:21: subjecting yourselves one to another in the fear of Christ [ASV].* Translations like the ASV rightly capture the descriptive, participial force of *upotassomenoi* – *subjecting yourselves* indicating an ongoing pattern of life. By itself, the word *upotassomenoi* < *upotassō* can be used in a variety of ways, but at its root it speaks of one who *places* [*tassō*] himself beneath [*upo*] another. This concept itself does not nullify the differentiated roles and offices of those who humble themselves and serve in this manner. For example, Luke reminds us that Christ *continued in subjection* [*upotassomenos*] to His parents as a youth (Luke 2:51), yet such submission and servitude in no way jeopardized His office as Lord and Savior. Neither does the call of submission in Ephesians 5:21 nullify the man's role as leader, the wife's role as his helpmeet, or the calling of children to obey their parents. The concept of mutual subjection and servitude is the very prescription to which Christ called all His disciples:

"Again and again our Lord, while on earth, emphasized this very thought, namely, that each disciple should be willing to be the least (Matt. 18:1-4; 20:28) and to wash the other disciples' feet (John 13:1-17). Substantially the same thought is also expressed in Rom. 12:10: 'in honor preferring one another' and in Phil. 2:3: '(doing) nothing from selfish ambition or from empty conceit, but in humble-mindedness each counting the other better than himself.'...the thought of the passage recalls what the apostle had said earlier in this same letter: 'with all lowliness and meekness, with longsuffering, enduring one another in love, making every effort to preserve the unity imparted by the Spirit by means of the bond (consisting in) peace' (Ephesians 4:2, 3). Paul knew by experience what would happen in a church when this rule is disobeyed (1 Cor. 1:11, 12; 3:1-9; 11:17-22; 14:26-33)."[245]

Our ultimate subjection to Christ must lead us to a humble subjection and servitude to one another, each according to our respective roles in life *in the fear of Christ.* To the extent that we can grow and excel in this, Christ will be exalted and all competing idols will be mortified. By this, households and churches will increase in the unspeakable privilege of heralding Christ (*Solus Christus*) and His precious word (*Sola Scriptura*).

May the Lord grant us all the grace needed to serve our risen Savior, reverently and with joy inexpressible.[246]

Soli Deo Gloria

---

[245] William Hendriksen, <u>New Testament Commentary</u> – Exposition of Ephesians, (Grand Rapids: Baker Books, 1996), 243.
[246] 1 Peter 1:8.

MY BANNER IS CHRIST

APPENDIX III

THOMAS MANTON'S

EPISTLE TO THE

READER

Mr. Thomas Manton's Epistle to the Reader

CHRISTIAN READER,

I CANNOT suppose thee to be such a stranger in England as to be ignorant of the general complaint concerning the decay of the power of godliness, and more especially of the great corruption of youth. Wherever thou goest, thou wilt hear men crying out of bad children and bad servants; whereas indeed the source of the mischief must be sought a little higher: it is bad parents and bad masters that make bad children and bad servants; and we cannot blame so much their untowardness, as our own negligence in their education.

The devil hath a great spite at the kingdom of Christ, and he knoweth no such compendious way to crush it in the egg, as by the perversion of youth, and supplanting family-duties. He striketh at all those duties which are publick in the assemblies of the saints; but these are too well guarded by the solemn injunctions and dying charge of Jesus Christ, as that he should ever hope totally to subvert and undermine them; but at family duties he striketh with the more success, because the institution is not so solemn, and the practice not so seriously and conscientiously regarded as it should be, and the omission is not so liable to notice and public censure. Religion was first hatched in families, and there the devil seeketh to crush it; the families of the Patriarchs were all the Churches God had in the world for the time; and therefore, (I suppose,) when Cain went out from Adam's family, he is said to go out from the face of the Lord, Gen. 4:16. Now, the devil knoweth that this is a blow at the root, and a ready way to prevent the succession of Churches: if he can subvert families, other societies and communities will not long flourish and subsist with any power and vigor; for there is the stock from whence they are supplied both for the present and future.

For the present: A family is the seminary of Church and State; and if children be not well principled there, all miscarrieth: a fault in the first concoction is not mended in the second; if youth be bred ill in the family, they prove ill in Church and Commonwealth; there is the first making or marring, and the presage of their future lives to be thence taken, Prov. 20:11. By family discipline, officers are trained up for the Church, 1 Tim. 3:4, One that ruleth well his own house, etc.; and there are men bred up in subjection and obedience. It is noted, Acts 21:5, that the disciples brought Paul on his way with their wives and children; their children probably are mentioned, to intimate, that their parents would, by their own example and affectionate farewell to Paul, breed them up in a way of reverence and respect to the pastors of the Church.

For the future: It is comfortable, certainly, to see a thriving nursery of young plants, and to have hopes that God shall have a people to serve him when we are dead and gone: the people of God comforted themselves in that, Ps. 102:28, The Children of thy servants shall continue, etc.

Upon all these considerations, how careful should ministers and parents be to train up young ones whilst they are yet pliable, and, like wax, capable of any form and impression, in the knowledge and fear of God; and betimes to instil the principles of our most holy faith, as they are drawn into a short sum in Catechisms, and so altogether laid in the view of conscience! Surely these seeds of truth planted in the field of memory, if they work nothing else, will at least be a great check and bridle to them, and, as the casting in of cold water doth stay the boiling of the pot, somewhat allay the fervours of youthful lusts and passions.

I had, upon entreaty, resolved to recommend to thee with the greatest earnestness the work of catechising, and, as a meet help, the usefulness of this book, as thus printed with the Scriptures at large: but meeting with a private letter of a very learned and godly divine, wherein that work is excellently done to my hand, I shall make bold to transcribe a part of it, and offer it to publick view.

The author having bewailed the great distractions, corruptions, and divisions that are in the Church, he thus represents the cause and cure: Among others, a principal cause of these mischiefs is the great and common neglect of the governors of families, in the discharge of that duty which they owe to God for the souls that are under their charge, especially in teaching them the doctrine of Christianity. Families are societies that must be sanctified to God as well as Churches; and the governors of them have as truly a charge of the souls that are therein, as pastors have of the Churches. But, alas, how little is this considered or regarded! But while negligent ministers are (deservedly) cast out of their places, the negligent masters of families take themselves to be almost blameless. They offer their children to God in baptism, and there they promise to teach them the doctrine of the gospel, and bring them up in the nurture of the Lord; but they easily promise, and easily break it; and educate their children for the world and the flesh, although they have renounced these, and dedicated them to God. This covenant-breaking with God, and betraying the souls of their children to the devil, must lie heavy on them here or hereafter. They beget children, and keep families, merely for the world and the flesh: but little consider what a charge is committed to them, and what it is to bring up a child for God, and govern a family as a sanctified society.

O how sweetly and successfully would the work of God go on, if we would but all join together in our several places to promote it!

Men need not then run without sending to be preachers; but they might find that part of the work that belongeth to them to be enough for them, and to be the best that they can be employed in. Especially women should be careful of this duty; because as they are most about their children, and have early and frequent opportunities to instruct them, so this is the principal service they can do to God in this world, being restrained from more publick work. And doubtless many an excellent magistrate hath been sent into the Commonwealth, and many an excellent pastor into the Church, and many a precious saint to heaven, through the happy preparations of a holy education, perhaps by a woman that thought herself useless and unserviceable to the Church. Would parents but begin betimes, and labour to affect the hearts of their children with the great matters of everlasting life, and to acquaint them with the substance of the doctrine of Christ, and, when they find in them the knowledge and love of Christ, would bring them then to the pastors of the Church to be tried, confirmed, and admitted to the further privileges of the Church, what happy, well-ordered Churches might we have! Then one pastor need not be put to do the work of two or three hundred or thousand governors of families, even to teach their children those principles which they should have taught them long before; nor should we be put to preach to so many miserable ignorant souls, that be not prepared by education to understand us; nor should we have need to shut out so many from holy communion upon the account of ignorance, that yet have not the grace to feel it and lament it, nor the wit and patience to wait in a learning state, till they are ready to be fellow-citizens with the saints, and of the household of God. But now they come to us with aged self-conceitedness, being past children, and yet worse than children still; having the ignorance of children, but being overgrown the teachableness of children; and think themselves wise, yea, wise enough to quarrel with the wisest of their teachers, because they have lived long enough to have been wise, and the evidence of their knowledge is their aged ignorance; and they are readier to flee in our faces for Church privileges, than to learn of us, and obey our instructions, till they are prepared for them, that they may do them good; like snappish curs, that will snap us by the fingers for their meat, and snatch it out of our hands; and not like children, that stay till we give it them. Parents have so used them to be unruly, that ministers have to deal but with too few but the unruly. And it is for want of this laying the foundation well at first, that professors themselves are so ignorant as most are, and that so many, especially of the younger sort, do swallow down almost any error that is offered them, and follow any sect of dividers that will entice them, so it be but done with earnestness and plausibility. For, alas! though by the grace of God their hearts may be changed in an hour, (whenever they understand but the essentials of the faith,) yet their understandings must have time and diligence to furnish them with such knowledge as must stablish them, and fortify them against deceits. Upon these, and many the like considerations, we should entreat all Christian families to take more pains in this necessary work, and to get better acquainted with the substance of Christianity. And, to that end, (taking along some moving treatises to awake the heart,) I know not what work should be fitter for their use, than that compiled by the Assembly at Westminster; a Synod of as godly, judicious divines, (notwithstanding all the bitter words which they have received from discontented and self-conceited men,) I verily think, as ever England saw. Though they had the unhappiness to be employed in calamitous times, when the noise of wars did stop men's ears, and the licentiousness of wars did set every wanton tongue and pen at liberty to reproach them, and the prosecution and event of those wars did exasperate partial discontented men to dishonour themselves by seeking to dishonour them; I dare say, if in the days of old, when councils were in power and account, they had had but such a council of bishops, as this of presbyters was, the fame of it for learning and holiness, and all ministerial abilities, would, with very great honour, have been transmitted to posterity.

I do therefore desire, that all masters of families would first study well this work themselves, and then teach it their children and servants, according to their several capacities. And, if they once understand these grounds of religion, they will be able to read other books more understandingly, and hear sermons more profitably, and confer more judiciously, and hold fast the doctrine of Christ more firmly, than ever you are like to do by any other course. First, let them read and learn the Shorter Catechism, and next the Larger, and lastly, read the Confession of Faith.

Thus far he, whose name I shall conceal, (though the excellency of the matter, and present style, will easily discover him,) because I have published it without his privity and consent, though, I hope, not against his liking and approbation. I shall add no more, but that I am, Thy servant, in the Lord's work,

Thy servant,
  in the Lord's work,
    THOMAS MANTON

MY BANNER IS CHRIST

INDEX

9 781935 358107

A
6 In all thy
7 Be not wi
evil: 8 It will
Honor Jeho
all thine incre
thy vats shall
the chastenin
For whom Jeho
in whom he
wisdom, And th
gaining of it is b
thereof than fine
none of the thing
her. 16 Length of
riches
o

1. All Nations Under God: The Doctrine of Chri
Defended, and Applied [ISBN: 978-1-935358-03

2. The First Institution: A Theological and Practic
Institution of Marriage and Family [ISBN: 978-1-9

3. Indeed, has Paul Really Said?: A Critique of N.T. \
[ISBN: 978-1-935358-02-2].

4. Altar to an Unknown Love: Rob Bell, C.S. Lewis, an
of Man [ISBN: 978-1-935358-08-4].

5. The Fallible Prophets of New Calvinism: An Analysis,
Concerning the Contemporary Doctrine of Fallible Prop

CPSIA information
Printed in the USA
BVOW02s195629
434466BV